Editorial Project Management

Editorial Project Management

With exercises and model answers

Barbara Horn

HORN EDITORIAL BOOKS

First published in Great Britain in 2006 by Horn Editorial Books,
32 Greenway Close, London N20 8EN

ISBN-13: 978-0-9553404-0-6
ISBN-10: 0-9553404-0-3

A CIP catalogue record for this work can be obtained
from the British Library

Typeset in 11/14 Sabon by M Rules
Printed and bound in Great Britain by
Biddles, 24 Rollesby Road, King's Lynn, Norfolk

Contents

Acknowledgements

This book is based on *Editorial Project Management by Distance Learning* (Publishing Training Centre), which I wrote in 2003. Writing both has been a collaborative process. Throughout my career in publishing I have learned from my colleagues, and continue to do so. I am especially grateful to Solveig Gardner-Servian for her excellent editing and for providing much-needed moral support. I am also particularly grateful to David Bann for information about and advice on production matters, Julia Silk for meticulous and thoughtful proofreading, and to Michèle Clarke for the index. Special thanks to Mike Hauser and Fred Riggey of M Rules for their patience, advice and excellent workmanship, and to Richard Johnson for the cover design and general help and guidance over many years.

I am grateful to the publishers who have given their kind permission to use copyright material, and to those publishers who helped me to track down some elusive copyright owners. The errors in the texts, introduced for the purpose of the exercises, are mine.

Every effort has been made to obtain permission to reproduce copyright material, but there may be cases where I have been unable to trace a copyright holder. I would be happy to correct any omissions in future printings.

Exercise 3.2 is based on information in *The Complete Manual of Fitness and Well-Being*, New York, Viking Press, 1984, and Jane Kirby and David Joachim, *Eat Up, Slim Down*, London, Rodale, 2002. The text in Exercise 6.2 is based on P. Francis Hunt, *Discovering Botany*, London, Longman, 1979. The text used in Exercise 6.3 is adapted from David G. Smith (ed.), *The Cambridge Encyclopedia of Earth Sciences*, Cambridge, CUP, 1981. The extract for Exercise 6.4 is adapted from the index in Andrew Sherratt (ed.), *The Cambridge Encyclopedia of Archaeology*, CUP, Cambridge, 1980.

Before you begin

The best way to work on a project is to identify the subject clearly, check that you have the appropriate resources to do the job, and establish what the intended outcome is, so let's do that.

What editorial project managers do

Editorial project managers are responsible for coordinating all the work on a publication from receipt of text, if not earlier, to publication. The principles of the job are the same regardless of the content of the publication; whether the publication is a new book or a reprint, or a journal, report, or in-house magazine; or whether the final output is printed on paper, produced on a tape or disk, or displayed on a web site:

* Assess the materials so that you can plan what needs to be done and how to do it.
* Analyse, and, if necessary, revise the schedule and budget so that you can ensure that they are adequate to produce work of the required quality.
* Choose the most appropriate people to work on the project.
* Brief the team members to enable them to do their work to the required standard.
* Supervise the work to ensure that schedules are met, budgets maintained and quality delivered.
* Establish, maintain and facilitate communications between everyone involved in the project.
* Provide feedback to the team, acknowledging work done well and providing constructive criticism of shortcomings, to build a good working relationship and a strong team.

What you need to know

Editorial project managers do not necessarily do any of the specific project work but they have to know enough about how each aspect of it is done in order to brief and supervise the work of others. Therefore, the book assumes that you have some experience in publishing and:

* understand the basic role of authors, commissioning editors, copy-editors, proofreaders, indexers, picture researchers, designers, illustrators, and production managers;
* are familiar with the principles of editing and marking up copy;
* know the standard proofreading symbols and how they are used;
* can collate proofs;
* know the basic rules of copyright;
* understand the stages of production;
* have access to and can use a computer and the Internet.

Computer and information technology have changed, and might continue to change, the way in which everyone on a project works, so you have to keep yourself up to date. However, regardless of the tools we use, the principle stages of a project remain the same:

1 Project proposed, costed and publication date agreed before acceptance
2 Authors' materials received
3 Authors' materials edited and marked up
4 Content designed
5 Textual matter typeset, illustrations scanned
6 Proofs produced and read
7 Proofs corrected
8 Publication printed and bound, or content uploaded

There can be some minor variation in the order of the stages – for example, the design can be done before the writing, simultaneously with the editing or after the editing – and there can be some additional stages, such as indexing and illustrating, as well as a number of revised proof stages, but none of the principle stages can be omitted.

Which production route will be taken is usually decided when the proposal is being evaluated; the project manager must ensure that the materials are suitable for the chosen route or that the route is changed to accommodate the nature of the materials. Most, but still not all, texts are delivered electronically. Whether those electronic files are suitable for use in editing or typesetting, or whether the text must be rekeyed, can affect schedules and budgets. Similarly, whether illustrations are submitted in digital form or have to be scanned, and whether film or digital files will be used to make the printing plates, will also affect schedules and budgets.

Who are the members of the team? Job titles vary from firm to firm: a publisher here may be a commissioning editor there or an acquisitions editor somewhere else; one company's production editor is another's production controller and a third's production manager; a managing editor might mean a project manager in some houses; and so on. In this book I use 'commissioning editor' for the person who initiates or acquires a project for the publishing house, 'project manager' for the person who sees the project through all its stages to publication, 'copy-editor' for the person who works on the text and ancillary materials to make the author's message clear to the reader, 'typesetter' for the person who does the typesetting and 'designer' for the person responsible for design work even if they are the same person, and 'production manager' for the person in charge of the manufacturing stages.

What you will learn

Editorial Project Management will guide you through acquiring the skills you need and the information underlying them in seven chapters, with these unsurprising titles: Scheduling, Budgeting, Assessing projects, Managing resources, Briefing, Supervising, and Feedback. Each chapter has three to five self-marking exercises to help you to test your understanding, and there is a glossary of important terms. You might want to photocopy some of the exercises to a larger size to make it easier to work on them. You may, of course, do that, but please remember that every page in the book is in copyright and may be photocopied only for your personal use.

Because books, particularly illustrated ones, are among the most complex types of projects, they are the basis of the skills and processes described. The principles are the same for other and simpler types of publications. Although these principles transcend national boundaries, it is not possible to make a book that deals with schedules and budgets truly international. In this book the dates for public holidays are based on those in the United Kingdom. Currency symbols have been omitted to avoid distraction, and the amounts are just notional.

One of the most important skills of any manager is communication. The book emphasizes when, why, and how to communicate, but it cannot test your ability or willingness to do so. That is your responsibility and one of the keys to your success.

1 Scheduling

A schedule is a framework of time and activities. Governed by when the manuscript is due and when the document will be published, it allocates periods of time between those two dates for the work to be done. A 'good' schedule allows sufficient time to enable everyone involved to produce work to the required standard within normal working hours. That's worth rereading, with emphasis on 'sufficient time', 'required standard', and 'normal working hours'. Schedules that do not allow enough time mean either that people will have to work overtime or that the required standard will not be met. People might have to work overtime when a crisis occurs, but that should be the exception rather than the rule. One of the project manager's main responsibilities is to ensure that schedules are adequate and are maintained. To do that, you need to understand how they are constructed and how they can be analysed and manipulated.

Time and processes

Once upon a time schedules were always worked out by the production department, because the physical specifications of a publication – its format, extent, number of words, number and type of illustrations, and type of binding – and its print run determine, then as now, the amount of time required for each manufacturing stage. Today, when some of the production processes are carried out by editors or designers, in-house or freelance, schedules may be initiated in either the editorial or the production department, or each might schedule the stages it controls; wherever the schedule originates, it is essential that all departments involved are consulted and agree to it.

There are many ways of producing a publication today. For example, authors are likely to produce the text on a computer and send it to their publisher on a CD or by e-mail, although a few might send only hard copy. The editor might edit on hard copy and input changes to the electronic files (e-files), or send the edited hard copy and e-files – or just the edited hard copy – to a typesetter, who will produce proofs. To ensure quality and efficiency, all but the shortest documents are best proofread on paper, although transferring the marks to PDFs on-screen saves time in sending proofs between proof-reader, project manager, and typesetter. The printer will be sent e-files to make the printing plates. These are usually PDFs for text-only books, and application files (such as Quark or InDesign), fonts and high-resolution files of pictures (for example TIFFs or JPEGs) for illustrated books. For illustrated books, the printer will produce a plotter proof for checking the imposition of pages before making the plates. (Film is rarely used now; when it is, the final film proof used for checking imposition is called an Ozalid, dyeline or blues.) Some processes take more time than others, and the location of some suppliers might require more time for transport of materials, so it is essential for the production path to be determined before the final schedule is decided.

The critical path

The typical schedule is based on the critical path of production: the chain of events that determines the minimum amount of time needed to complete the task. So, whereas there are many activities involved in producing a publication, the critical path refers only to those that must be finished before the next one can begin; for example, the text must be typeset before it can be proofread.

Exercise 1.1: Identifying the critical path of production for a novel, from manuscript due to publication date

Here is a list, in random order, of activities involved in producing a book. Select the activities that comprise the critical path of a novel from the date the manuscript is received. Write down each link of the chain and connect it to the next link with an arrow.

e-files to printer	text in
jacket/cover blurb to design	clear text permissions
printed jacket/cover in	brief illustrator
index out for typesetting	picture list in
return first proofs	printing

pass proofs for press	books delivered
index in	final artwork in
brief picture researcher	jacket/cover proof in
approve illustrator's visuals	copy-edit text
make plates	plotter proofs in and out
first proofs in	clear photo permissions
jacket/cover design in	bound books dispatched
illustration proofs out	index proof out
brief designer	illustration proofs in
typeset text	publication date
initial type and page design in	photos and artwork to production
index proof in	
second proofs in	

Notice that the list does not include 'read proofs' or 'collate proofs'. The first is an assumed activity within the stage 'first proofs in', and the second does not happen in all cases. You will see how to annotate the schedules with this kind of information later in the chapter.

Look at the activities that do not appear on the model answer. Although they are involved in producing a book, they do not determine the next step. For example, initial page design can be done before the text is copy-edited or after; it can even be done before the text is in house, and in some houses it doesn't need to be done at all, because there is a single design for all texts in a particular list. Similarly, although the cover or jacket needs to be finished at least by the time the book is printing, it can be produced much earlier; in fact, it has its own critical path. Because they are not on the text's critical path, these activities often do not appear on production schedules – but they must appear on your schedules.

Now look at Exercise 1.1 again and identify the critical path of production from manuscript to publication for a work of illustrated non-fiction.

Compare your answer with that for Exercise 1.1. It should be almost identical; the only difference is that an illustrated book might include dates for checking a plotter proof between 'e-files to printer' and 'make plates'. Are you surprised that this is the only difference? You knew, of course, that the critical path did not include the jacket or cover and the initial page design, but did you realize that all the stages up to passing proofs for press would be exactly the same as for an unillustrated work? The very important point here is that the other elements involved in producing an illustrated book are not part of the main critical path; they have their own critical paths, and these can overlap some stages in the main path. Whereas the schedule for the main critical path is determined by the dates for receipt of manuscript and publication, the schedules for the subsidiary paths may be determined by non-consecutive points on the main path.

Subsidiary critical paths

Let's look, for example, at producing an index. We can identify the stages on its critical path as:

brief indexer → index in→ copy-edit index → typeset index → index proof in → pass proof for press

All the stages are linked, the end of one signalling the beginning of another. The compilation of the index usually begins as soon as page proofs are available – a point on the main path. Its proof should be passed for press at the same time as the rest of the book – obviously another point on the main path. If this end date is missed, it could affect the main critical path, delaying the printing.

The jacket, or cover, is another example of an element with its own critical path:

brief jacket designer → jacket roughs in → jacket design approved → final artwork → jacket proof → jacket proof approved → jackets printed and delivered

Once again, there are other activities involved – writing the blurb and other copy, providing illustrations in some cases, providing the bar code and ISBN – but their start dates are not determined by the end date of another activity on the path, and their end dates do not signal the beginning of the next stage. They can overlap with some stages on the jacket's critical path: for example, the blurb can be provided when the designer is briefed or when the roughs are approved. It is your responsibility to decide when these tasks should start and when they must be completed.

Similarly, you must ensure that production knows the extent of the book and can advise the jacket designer of the spine width before the jacket artwork is finalized. In non-fiction publishing it is usual to determine the page extent before the proposal is approved, but in fiction it is not possible to know the extent until the text is set. In the latter case, you can annotate your schedule to remind yourself to get this information from production when the first proofs are in.

Although in book publishing it is rare now for illustrations to be proofed separately from text, 'rare' is not the same as 'never', and this generality might not apply to all types of publishing. The reference to the illustration proofs is to keep you aware.

Allocating time

When schedules are being created, it is standard practice to start at the end – the publication date – and work backwards to the date the text is due. The reason for this is simple: every publisher – whether of books or journals, reports, newsletters or leaflets – has a set (or, at

MS in	4 Jan
MS to typesetting	8 Feb
First proofs in	2 Mar
Proofs returned	22 Mar
Second proofs in	6 Apr
Proofs passed for press	20 Apr
Copies in	24 May
Publication	6 July

Figure 1.1 A typical production schedule for a text-only book. Illustrated books might also show dates for checking plotter proofs.

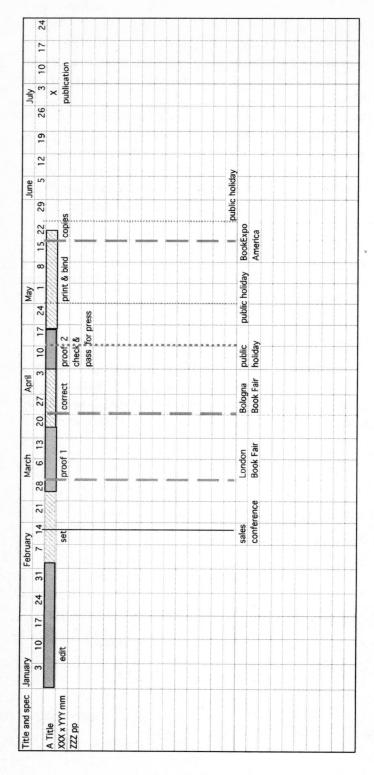

Figure 1.2 Global schedule. Vertical lines highlight dates that can affect working time. The title and relevant specifications are given in the first column, and the critical path is plotted using one colour or pattern for editorial stages and another for production stages.

least, preferred) period of time between receiving copies in the office or warehouse and distribution for publication. The time required for the production, or manufacturing, processes is also predetermined; as mentioned earlier, it can be accurately assessed from a book's specifications. The time remaining between the first production process and the receipt of manuscript is then allocated to the pre-press stages. You must check that the time allocated to each stage on the critical path is adequate (see Chapter 3), and negotiate adjustments if it is not. At this point you need to see the scheduling information in detail.

Seeing the complete picture

Production schedules are sometimes just a vertical list of dates on the critical path (Fig. 1.1). In order to manage projects you need to be able to see all the critical and subsidiary paths of each one simultaneously, and you need to be able to see all the projects for which you are responsible at the same time. Vertical schedules usually do not allow you to do this, so use a single horizontal form on which you can plot the schedules of all your projects. Figure 1.2 shows you a global schedule form on which the critical path for the same book has been plotted. The path follows time along the horizontal scale, while the titles, and their specifications or other information about them, can be written in the first column. You can create a global schedule form on a computer with a spreadsheet program or special software, or you can do it using pens and paper.

Exercise 1.2: Plotting the schedule of a book and its jacket

Create a global schedule form like the one in Figure 1.2, using the dates given there. Plot the schedule of *A History of Philanthropy*, a text-only work 256 pages long, including references to copyright sources and an index. The format is 266 × 155 mm, and the jacket will be typographic. The author, who has been working on the book for nearly two years, will e-mail the text, and the typesetter will input all the editorial changes and proof corrections.

1 It is important to see schedules against the time available for work.

* Using a highlighter, draw vertical lines down the form to indicate the public holidays, making the thickness of the

lines reflect the number of days affected. In real life, you would, of course, record the actual date of public holidays, but for the purpose of this exercise, use the dates in Figure 1.2. Label the holidays at the bottom of the line.

- Using a different coloured highlighter, draw vertical lines to indicate major book fairs. In real life you can use the Internet to check the dates for such events that affect your work, but, again, for the purpose of this exercise include the fairs and dates shown in Figure 1.2, and label each one at the bottom.
- Using the second highlighter again, indicate a sales conference in the second week in February and one the second week in September.

2 Use the dates below to plot the critical path of the book across a single line, using one colour for editorial stages and another for production stages. Underneath this line, draw any subsidiary paths you think necessary, and annotate them.

MS in . . . . 10 April

MS out . . . . 12 May

First page proofs in . . . . 5 June

Proofs returned . . . . 23 June

Revised proofs in . . . . 10 July

Proofs passed for press . . . . 21 July

Copies in . . . . 28 Aug

Publication . . . . 5 Oct

The model answer can't show it, but you should have included some time for your personal holidays. It is very important to do this on global schedule forms so that you can see what stage projects will be at while you're away and make plans for delegating responsibilities if necessary. It is equally important to make sure that you take your holiday time. Whether you work in-house or freelance, try to operate on the principle of making your work fit in with your life, not letting your life be controlled by your work.

Checking the detail

In the exercise, notice that two public holidays occur during the period allocated to editing. In your real job you would need to assess whether, despite the loss of these working days, there is still enough time to do the copy-editing to the required quality during normal working hours; if there isn't, you would need to adjust the schedule. You should also note when sales conferences occur and whether they will have any impact on personnel or processes for which you are responsible.

In most book publishing, the first proofs are usually read by the author, whose contract stipulates the time allowed (often two weeks), as well as by a proofreader. The marks and other changes on the two sets of proofs are collated by the copy-editor or the proofreader, or, sometimes, by the project manager. This part of the critical path has been annotated because you need to be aware of the time allocated for these parts of the task so that you can:

- tell the author when the proofs are coming and when they need to be returned;
- make sure a proofreader is lined up to do the work and knows the schedule;
- remind the person collating the proofs when this has to be done and the proofs returned.

It is always wise to allow a little time at each stage, relative to the the size of the job, for contingencies – unforeseeable problems – and a little time between receiving materials and sending them to the next stage so that you can check the quality of the work and prepare any covering letters, briefs or memos. You also have to consider how materials will be sent: will they be delivered electronically at all stages or do you have to allow time for them to be sent by post or courier?

The schedule says copies will be in on 28 August. However, this is marked as another public holiday on the model answer. In such a situation, although you assume the copies will be delivered the next working day, you should draw this to the production manager's attention in case there are ramifications of which you are unaware; for example, the delivery is arriving from abroad and the supplier is not aware of the holiday, or adjustments to procedures in the warehouse or distribution centre might be necessary.

The brief says there are references to copyright sources, which indicates that permissions need to be cleared. Generally, permissions should be cleared by the time first proofs are returned for correction. Although it is possible to wait until later, you run the risk that some permissions will not be granted and sections of the book will have to be altered, causing delay and additional expense. The later in the process the delay occurs, the more expensive it will be. This is a task that does not have to be done all at once and can start as soon as the manuscript is received. Of course, you need to decide who will be responsible for doing it and make sure there is sufficient time in his or her part of the schedule (see Chapter 4).

The index has to be passed for press with the text proofs. Working backwards from that date, you need to allow for the possibility that a revised proof will be needed; this is fairly unusual but, if necessary, can be produced and proofread quite quickly, as the index is only eight pages long. Similarly, proofreading the first proof of the index can be done in less than a week, and so can the setting. That leaves about four weeks from when the first proofs are in until the index goes for setting. Within that period you have to allow time for creating and editing the index. How long an index takes to create depends on the length and complexity of the book, and the type and complexity of the index. For a straightforward text, allow 8–10 pages an hour. Here, initially allowing three weeks for the index to be created and one week for editing should be adequate. If when you discuss the job with the indexer and editor, you find that either of them wants more time, you can check exactly how long to allow for setting, and you can trim the proofreading time if necessary.

No time frame was given for producing the jacket. When did you think it had to be finished? Jackets and covers are sales tools, and the marketing and sales department will have an ideal date by which it wants jackets available. It is often between six and nine months before publication. For many books that can mean as soon as the manuscript is received, and for some books, including this one, even before that. Notice when the sales conferences are. The one in February is when the sales department will want jackets for books being published from July to December. September is too late: having jackets only three weeks before publication does not allow the sales team sufficient time to sell the book properly. In theory, covers or jackets can be started as soon as the title and author's name are confirmed. Those that are only typographic can be completed more quickly than those that require illustrations. The designer could be briefed in the preceding December or in January to produce this typographic jacket in time for the sales conference. In your real job, find out when the sales conferences are – they are scheduled months in advance – and what sales period they relate to; then check with the designer and the production manager about the amount of time they need, so that you can always plan to have relevant materials ready in time, without panic or stress.

The length of time between passing the revised proofs for press and the publication date depends on various factors, such as the extent of the book, whether it is monochrome or full colour, the print run, where the printer is in relation to the publisher and whether the proofs are being sent as hard copy or electronically, or are simply being approved by e-mail. The production manager will estimate the printing time based on the specifications of the job and will know the time needed for getting bound copies from the printer and binder to the warehouse, and the length of time before publication that copies have to be in the warehouse. In the exercises in this book that information will be provided. On the job, you must make sure you get this information and understand the criteria on which it is based.

Illustrated books

So far we have considered only the elements in an unillustrated book. Illustrated publications include artwork or photos, or both. In each case you need to work out the chain of activities that form the critical path. Remember, the end of each activity must signal the beginning of another. Some people find it easiest to work out the chain from the outcome: what must happen before this can happen? Others prefer to start at the beginning: what happens next? You can use one method to check the other, to make sure that each step is linked to the one before it and the one after it.

Check these subsidiary paths:

artwork list → artwork brief → illustrator's visuals → visuals approved → final artwork

picture list → picture researcher's brief → preliminary selection → final selection

picture list → photographer's brief → final photographs

In preparing schedules for illustrated books, find out whether you will be asked to check the plotter proof – it is not always the case. Usually, you will be told to return the proof the day after receipt.

Different ways to proceed

Who sizes the illustrations, and at what stage, varies. In some houses, editors size illustrations during the editing; in others, designers size illustrations when they are composing the first page proofs; and sometimes production staff or typesetters do this job. Most photographs are available in digital format and can be dropped into place as the pages are created. Prints and transparencies, and artwork that is not created on a computer, must be scanned and digitized. Some publishers have their own high-quality scanners, and others send the work to an external supplier. Like other aspects of a proof, the illustrations need to be checked and marked for correction.

Whether you read the paths shown above from the beginning or from the end, you can see that each step is linked. Remember, however, that there might be other activities involved in each one that are not part of its critical path and for which you have to plan.

There might also be other critical or subsidiary paths. For example, a project might require permissions to be cleared; or have a number of products: a main book, a supplementary book, an audio cassette or CD, a related web site or merchandise. Or it might be a simultaneous co-edition, and require a path for sending materials to and receiving materials from co-publishers. In each case you must analyse the process to determine what the linked stages are so that you can allocate the appropriate amount of time to each of them.

Exercise 1.3: Creating a schedule for an illustrated book

It is the end of September. You have just been told that *Art: 1975–2000*, by Clive Haystacks, is to be published on the third Thursday in September next year to coincide with an important exhibition. Dr Haystacks, a professor of art history, has written several popular books, and always turns in a complete picture list and text on time. His approach is to look at art in relation to its period, making reference to contemporaneous events and materials such as books, films, letters and diaries. He has been working on the book since January last year and is due to deliver hard copy and e-files of the manuscript on 13 February.

The specifications are:

* Format: 290 × 225 mm
* Extent: 256 pages
* Printing: 4/4
* Binding: hardcover with 4-colour jacket
* Words: 150,000
* Illustrations 280 photos

The designer will be setting the book and making proof corrections. He has estimated four weeks from manuscript to first proof, including any scanning of illustrations that might be required, and two weeks for making corrections and supplying revised proofs. He has allowed eight pages for the index. Production allows two weeks for editorial to correct the proofs and one week to collate those corrections with its own, so that these proofs are returned at the same time as text is passed for press. Printing will take four weeks and transport to the warehouse will take one week.

Plan the schedule on a global schedule form, showing all the critical paths and annotating any of them where you think it will help you to manage your resources. Include book fairs, holidays and sales conferences at about the same time as those in Figure 1.2, adding any holidays not shown there.

Did you remember to include your own holiday? On the model answer one public holiday occurs during typesetting, one public holiday during proofreading and the period for creating the index, and another during the time for checking second proofs and reading the index proof. On the job you should check with all relevant personnel – for example, the designer, production manager, copy-editor, proofreader, and indexer – that they are aware of any such conflicts and still have adequate time to complete their work. Remember, at each stage the schedule should also include a little contingency time and time for you to check work and prepare briefs.

Seeing implications

The book has a seven-month schedule. If jackets are wanted at least six months before publication, and certainly for the sales conference in February, you should plan work to begin as early as October of the current year to be ready in January of the next year. If a blad were also needed, it could be prepared at the same time. Because the text has been in development for so long, it should be possible to get the author to provide draft text and a list of images that will definitely be used, from which jacket and internal illustrations can be selected. Although the jacket and blad illustrations cannot be changed later, the text is a relatively inexpensive element and can be amended. Unfortunately, because jackets and blads are often seen as 'small' elements, it is assumed they don't take long to prepare and print, and so they are not always allowed optimum time. Plan to give every element sufficient time for the work to be done to the quality required without panic and undue haste. The model answer gives an idea of the time that might be taken; your job is always to check with all the personnel involved – the team members – the length of time needed for each stage.

The brief said the author will be making references to other sources, so you should have realized that clearing copyright permissions might be necessary. Remember, permissions should be cleared by the time first proofs are ready to be returned for correction.

Illustrations

In the exercise, all the illustrations are to be photos. Ideally, they should all go to the designer with the text. That means that the research, including preliminary and final selection, has to be completed by then. It is a good idea to annotate this line with the two selection dates so that you can see the effect if there is a delay in either of them.

You had to decide when the picture research should begin. The answer is 'as soon as possible', which means when the picture list is in. A delay in getting some of the original images will not always cause a delay in the schedule. Designers can use photocopies, if they are available, for sizing, but the originals must be available by the time the pages are are returned for correction. If photocopies are not available and the designer has to guess how much space to leave, the layout of the pages on which those photos occur, and perhaps others, might have to be revised.

In some instances the choice of which illustrations are to be used is dependent on the reproduction quality of the prints, transparencies or other originals, such as X-rays or CT scans. Then a delay in getting the images can have an impact on the schedule, if, for example, the originals are not, or require special work to make them, suitable for use.

The greater the number of illustrations that are not available until the first proofs are sent for correction, the longer it will take to produce the revised proofs, endangering the schedule and the budget. There is also the possibility that further corrections will be needed when the proofs of these late illustrations are seen for the first time, and if revising the layouts created new problems, such as orphans and widows, that need to be resolved. An extra proof stage will take more time and cost more money than planned. Even worse, every correction made is an opportunity for a new error to creep in, and a project can suddenly spiral out of control.

Commissioned photos should always be ready to go with the text for setting. You need to coordinate the schedule for photography with whoever is responsible for organizing and supervising the shoot – usually the designer or picture researcher – and the copy-editor if he or she is preparing the briefs. The briefs must be ready in advance of the shoot date so that materials, models and other personnel, and locations can be prepared.

When you are managing a project like this and the schedule is tight, think about getting the illustration list from the author before the text is due so that there is enough time for researching sourced photos, and for briefing and preparation for commissioned photography.

Schedules for commissioned artwork should be the same as for photos. It is true that because whoever briefs the artwork – you or the copy-editor – will determine its size and shape, and will probably have visuals, or roughs, from the illustrator, the designer can plan the pages without the final artwork. Then the final artwork must be in and approved by the time the first pages are returned for correction. However, as explained above, this creates more work at the correction stage, can lead to further corrections, and endangers the schedule and the budget.

Series and loose-leafs

Each book in a series should be plotted individually whether the publication dates are simultaneous or staggered, because you need to be able to monitor the teams and deal with any problems they might have individually. If estimates of time for one part of a critical path in one book prove inaccurate, decide whether the cause is particular to that volume or whether the problem is generic and you need to adjust that part of the schedule for the other books.

Loose-leaf publications are a continuous staggered series of publication. Like a book in a series, each tranche of text should be scheduled and monitored individually, and problems in one segment that are identified as generic should be corrected in the schedules for later segments.

No delays, please

Slippage, or delay in the schedule, is dreaded but not exactly rare. Publishing any commercial product late always means financial loss. In some cases, particularly educational publishing, it can result in loss of market share too, because buyers turn to a competitor's product when yours is not available, and then look first to that competitor for other products.

The cost of delays might also be personal. Producing any publication involves a number of individuals who operate as a team. There must be enough time for each team member to do his or her job. If one person takes longer than planned, it will affect other people on the critical path; perhaps they will have less time in which to complete their work, or will have to reorganize or change their suppliers. If they are freelance, they might have to turn away the work because it conflicts with other jobs, or they might have a gap because they turned away other work to be ready for the now delayed job. All these situations produce stress, and some can affect the relationships that these other people have with their suppliers. If many of your projects are subject to slippage, it will have a negative effect on your relationships with your colleagues.

Your job is to try to make sure there is no slippage, by planning schedules realistically – including contingency time – and monitoring them carefully. However well you do this, there will sometimes be delays: people get ill or have personal crises, authors and consultants might have to give priority to their regular jobs (this is particularly true in educational, legal and medical publishing), and equipment breaks down. As soon as you spot a potential delay you need to explain to the other team members what has happened or is going to happen, and work out how to deal with it. (Techniques for dealing with delays are covered in Chapter 6.)

A management tool

There are some people who say that plotting the schedules of their projects in this way is too time-consuming. Don't listen to them for even a minute. They are often the same people who are running around trying to deal with scheduling crises – late covers, late text, late illustrations, late proofs – that need never have arisen. A proper schedule is the foundation for success of each project. When you plot the schedules of all your projects showing the critical and subsidiary paths, you have a tool that helps you manage your resources and control your work. Here are seven ways to use the tool.

1 The schedule shows the dates relevant to each element of each project. Check with team members that the times allocated to each activity are realistic: that they allow the work to be done to the required quality within normal working hours (see Chapter 3). If time for any task is not adequate, and you cannot find ways to make it so and still maintain the publication date, it is your responsibility to report this to the commissioning editor or publisher. An unrealistic schedule will affect the budget or quality of the project.

2 Keep the global schedule where you can see it easily at all times. It is easy to create and update the schedule on a computer, using special project-management software or just a spreadsheet. You might be able to program the computer to remind you of key

dates, too. However, there might be many times a day when you need to refer to the global schedule or a part of it, so print out and keep an up-to-date copy where it is always visible to you.

3 Use the schedule to monitor the dates as the projects progress. You will be able to see at a glance the impact a delay in any area will have on the rest of the schedule. Your job will be to try to prevent the initial delay, or, if that's not possible, to negotiate how to compensate for it without affecting the publication date. Most importantly, seeing where the impact of a delay will be tells you which colleagues you must alert.

4 The schedule shows when holidays occur during the period allotted to any task. Check to see whether the time actually available for work is still adequate. If necessary, revise the time frame or the use of resources to avoid potential delays.

5 The global schedule shows you when you need to have people ready to do particular jobs. Use it to give yourself sufficient time to find the most appropriate copy-editor and proofreader, and other specialists needed, and to give these team members an estimate of when and for how long their services will be required. You can also annotate the paths to show when authors and consultants will be involved so that you can give them adequate notice and ensure their availability. On long projects it might be useful to annotate the schedule to show when key team members are not available.

6 As soon as you have plotted the schedule for a single project, check what materials will be needed for sales conferences and book fairs, so that you can plan when and by whom they will be prepared without delaying the other tasks.

7 When you have plotted the schedules of a number of projects, you will be able to see potential conflicts between them and plan how to avoid them. For example, a very important part of managing projects is checking the quality of the work done as it passes from one stage to the next. If handover stages of several projects are all going to be in the same week, you might try to stagger them so that one arrives the previous week, one early in the week and one later in the week, allowing you time to check each one without delaying the next stage.

2 Budgeting

A budget for a publication is very much like any other budget: an estimate of what it will cost to do or buy something of a particular quality set against the finances available. When you budget to buy a piece of furniture, for example, you are saying 'I can afford to pay this much for a piece of this quality.' Maybe you hope to spend less than you budgeted, regarding the budget figure as a maximum and a lower figure as more desirable. The difference between the two amounts is the contingency element. You might plan this amount to cover the cost of any expense you forgot to include or didn't foresee – delivery charges, perhaps. If you stay within your budget, you're fine. What is the consequence if you spend more than you planned? It depends on your circumstances, of course, but even if it isn't misery, as Mr Micawber predicts, it's still not good.

The budget for a publication is also based on an estimate of the maximum costs to achieve a particular qualitative result, and should include a contingency amount. Here, all costs that can be expected must be included and the contingency is for those items that couldn't be foreseen. Staying within the budget is not only happiness but it is also expected. Exceeding the budget is indeed misery, as we shall see.

Composition

The person responsible for initiating the project, the commissioning editor, creates the budget. An estimate of the costs is essential in deciding whether or not to proceed with an idea. As project manager, you might be asked to estimate certain costs or you might just be given a budget for a project. In either case you have to understand how the budget is composed, how to check it and how to maintain it.

Income

When you're budgeting for that furniture, where do you start? Do you decide what you want first and then do some research to find out how much you will have to pay, or do you determine how much you

19

RSP − % discount × domestic sales
+ RSP − % discount × export sales
= turnover
+ other income
= total income

Figure 2.1 Project budget: income

can afford to spend first and then see what you can get? Publishers have to look at the income a project will produce against the costs of creating it. They often start by setting the price they think the market will pay for a specific item, the recommended selling price (RSP). Unless they sell directly to the consumer, by direct mail or subscription for example, they will apply a discount to the RSP. There will be one discount for the home, or domestic, market and a higher discount for the export market. Publishers multiply the discounted price by the number of items they estimate they can sell in each market. The number of items available for sale is the print or product run minus a set number of copies, often referred to as 'freebies', that are given to the authors, sent out for review, distributed to sales personnel, and so forth. The money to be received from sales is turnover.

Publishers will examine other ways of making money from the project. For example, if the project is a hardback book, they may estimate income from selling the following rights:

• translation, or foreign language
• book club, paperback and electronic
• serial or excerpt
• broadcasting, film or cartoon strip
• merchandising

They'll add the amount from all these subsidiary rights to the turnover to get the total income (Fig. 2.1).

Direct costs and overheads

Having estimated the potential income, the commissioning editor is ready to estimate the expenditure necessary to produce the project. The more accurate and complete the commissioning editor is in specifying the project, the more likely it is that all the required direct costs will be included in the budget. Direct costs are those that are incurred in creating a specific title: in other words, money spent on that project only. Costs that cannot be attributed to a specific project are overheads, and are usually figured as a percentage of the project's turnover. Authors' fees or royalties and printing and binding, for example, are always direct costs. Electricity, rent, insurance, the salaries of all employees (some of whom do not work on any specific project) and other costs of running the company are overheads. Some activities might be direct costs in one company, or only on a particular project, and overheads in another.

Exercise 2.1: Establishing direct costs and overheads.

Images & Ideas is a company that publishes light fiction in the same single format it has used for 30 years and individually designed illustrated non-fiction. The novels are project managed, edited, and typeset and corrected in-house; proofreading and all other work is done by external suppliers. The non-fiction titles are project managed in-house, but all the work is done by external suppliers. From the items below, list the direct costs and overheads for *Moonlight Messenger*, a novel, and for *Creating Scented Gardens*, a book illustrated with photographs and artwork.

author	picture fees
artwork	picture research
binding	printing
book design	project management
commissioning	proof corrections
copy-editing	proofing
indexing	proofreading
jacket design	scanning illustrations
page make-up	typesetting
paper and other materials	

You can see that an illustrated book has many more tasks and costs than a text-only one, whether it is fiction or non-fiction, and you probably found it relatively easy to put the costs in the right categories. The cost of work done externally is always set against a specific project. When work is done in-house, the cost usually is part of the overheads, although in some firms staff keep time sheets so that their contribution can be costed against specific projects too.

In the exercise no cost is allocated for the book design of the novel because the company uses only one design, which may have been a single payment costed against its first title or is a small part of the overheads now, whereas the jacket design is specific to each title and is commissioned from a freelance designer. Similarly, there would be a single book-design cost for a series and individual costs for covers or jackets for each volume. Loose-leafs have single costs for page design and for the design of the cover of the folder or file.

Fixed and variable costs

Direct costs are themselves divided into 'fixed' and 'variable'. A fixed cost is one that is not affected by the print or product run: it is the same whether you produce one copy or thousands of copies. Type-setting, for example, is a fixed cost. Variable costs are those that are relative to the product run or the sales market. Paper and CDs are examples of a variable cost: the more copies you print, the more paper or CDs you need.

Photo and text permissions are variable costs, too, relative to the size of the product run and the markets in which the project is to be sold. When you are negotiating such fees, you refer to the market rights you need. For publications relevant only to the domestic market, the rights are bought for that country only – UK rights, for example. UK and Commonwealth rights are appropriate when a work will be sold in those member countries. When a project is suit-able for co-edition in several or all countries in a particular language group, the rights would be purchased for that language worldwide – world English-language rights or world French-language rights for example. When projects are suitable for co-edition in only a few countries, the individual language rights are bought; and when they are suitable for co-edition in many countries, world rights are needed. Generally, the wider the market, the higher the fee.

When creating the budget, it is important to consider the markets in which the project *might* be sold as well as those where it is certain to be sold. If a title has extensive international potential that might not be realized at the same time as domestic publication, it is usually less expensive, in actual terms as well as in administrative time and expense, to buy world rights initially rather than renegotiate rights for each new edition as it arises.

Exercise 2.2: Identifying fixed and variable costs

Here, again, are the costs associated with *Creating Scented Gardens*. This time separate them into fixed costs and variable costs.

author	picture fees
artwork	picture research
binding	printing
book design	project management
commissioning	proof corrections
copy-editing	proofing
indexing	proofreading
jacket design	scanning illustrations
page make-up	typesetting
paper and other materials	

That may have seemed an easy exercise but there are a couple of caveats, which relate to the costs for the author, artwork, and book and jacket design. If an author is paid a fee – as many authors of articles in journals or loose-leafs, chapters in multi-author books and illustrated books are – that is a fixed cost. If an author receives royalties, as most authors of fiction and many of non-fiction books do, that is a variable cost, dependent not only on how many copies are sold but also on where and at what discount.

The copyright of the index, artwork, book design, and jacket, cover or CD cover design belongs to the creators of those works. For the fees paid to be fixed costs, the contract with the supplier, which may be as simple as an order form, must indicate that the fee is either for the purchase of the copyright or for the licence to use the material in all current and future editions, which is virtually the same thing. Without such a written agreement, the illustrator or designer could ask for, and be entitled to, further payment for use of the material in co-editions and even revised editions.

Estimate forms

The commissioning editor gathers the estimated costs from relevant people, such as project managers, designers, and production managers. Companies design estimate request forms to try to make this procedure efficient and to ensure that no vital element is overlooked. The design of the forms varies from firm to firm – some contain basic editorial and design information that the production department uses to provide a detailed estimate of its costs, others include only the production estimate – but the similar contents reflect the elements common to producing particular products. Compare the examples in Figure 2.3 (pages 25–6). Notice that both include fees for editorial and design work, which indicates that the publishers are prepared to assign these as direct costs rather than overheads. Notice, too, that the forms vary in the amount of detail they provide for establishing the illustrations budget.

Calculating the margin

Just as publishers have lists that determine what subjects or types of books they will consider, they have financial guidelines that determine which projects they will publish. One financial guideline is the ratio of the net profit margin of the project to the total income, expressed as a percentage. The net profit margin is calculated by subtracting the direct costs and the overheads from the total income (Fig. 2.2). Publishers will have a minimum, or target, ratio, but might be willing to approve some projects that fall below it, because they are developing the author or the list, or because the work is an important contribution to a field of study

```
        RSP – % discount × domestic sales
      + RSP – % discount × export sales
      = turnover
      + other income
      = total income
      – direct costs
      = gross profit margin
      – overheads (set % of income)
      = net profit margin
```

Figure 2.2 Project budget: net profit margin

ESTIMATE REQUEST

Series _____

Title _____   Department_____

Author _____

Min quantity to quote   UK _____

                               Clubs _____

                               Editions _____

                               Total _____

Specifiation

TPS ×   mm   Landscape/Portrait

No. of words _____   Disk Yes/No

Make-up   Single column/double column/margin references/notes

Special fonts _____

No. pages   Prelims _____

                     Main text _____

                     Endmatter _____

                     Illustrations _____

                     Total _____   + colour pages = _____

Illustrations   No. colour _____   Cut-outs _____ %

                     No. b/w halftones _____   Cut-outs _____ %

                     No. b/w line _____

                     Total _____

How illustrations fall:

B/w   Integrated/Inserts × pp/Wraps × pp/Sections × pp

Colour   Integrated 4×1/4×4

                     Inserts × pp/Wraps × pp/Sections × pp

Jacket/Cover   No. colour illustrations   1-col/2-col/3-col/4-col/5-col

                     No. b/w illustrations _____

Endpapers   White/Coloured stock/Printed col x col

Binding   Cased/Limp/Other   Real cloth Yes/No/Other

Budgets

Author	Fee/Advance _____	Royalty _____	%HB _____	%PB
	Reprint fee own edn _____	Royalty _____	%HB _____	%PB
	Reprint fee co-edn _____	Royalty _____	%HB _____	%PB

Design fee _____

Pic fees _____   Domestic/World/Language

Copy-editing fee _____

Proofreading fee _____

Indexing fee _____

Sales/Dummy _____

Blads _____

Other (a/w etc.) _____

Figure 2.3 Sample estimate request forms

PRODUCTION ESTIMATE REQUEST

Date ....
Title ....
Series ....
ISBN ....
Author(s)...
Format × mm ....
Extent ....pp
Binding style...
Words ....

Artwork	Line	B/w half-tone	No. colour
Photos	B/w half-tone	Colour	
Illustrations	Integrated	Sections	
Cover	No. colours		
Text	No. colours		

Costs

Author ....
Contributors' fees ....
Editor's fees ....
Copy-editing ....
Proofreading ....
Advisors' fees ....
Indexing ....

Illustrators' fees ....
Picture researcher's fee ....
Photos ....
Cover/case artwork ....
Permissions fees ....
Total ....

Plant

Typesetting ....
Film ....
Printer/binder ....
Text paper ....
Endpaper material ....
Cover material ....
Case materials ....
Lamination ....

Page composition ....
Page correction ....
Scanning/wet proofs ....
Extra proofs ....
Blurb setting ....
Cover/case proofs ....
Misc extras ....
Total ....

Figure 2.3 continued

and, therefore, to their reputation. If they decide to accept projects that fall below the target ratio, it is usually only with the knowledge that there are other titles on the list that will achieve more than the target ratio. Falling below the target ratio is not the same as failing to break even or make a profit.

Some publishers divide the gross profit margin by the total income, and use this percentage as their guideline. However, this allows people to overlook the effect of overheads, and sometimes even to try to hide direct costs in overheads to make the project figures work. That can lead to trouble.

Exercise 2.3: The effect of rising overheads

Near End Publishers, a small company, needs to maintain a 50 per cent net profit margin as an average over its entire list. It works out its costings on the basis of overheads at 38 per cent of turnover. Schedules and budgets are tight and staff are warned of the dangers of exceeding either. To help maintain some endangered schedules, staff have relied on couriers, who were 0.25 per cent of overheads, to transport materials between the firm and all its suppliers, including foreign printers. At the end of the second financial quarter the accountant has found that the average impact the increased spending on couriers has had on overheads and net profit margins is shown by Project A. Forecast to earn 50,000 in home and export sales, it apparently did not exceed its direct cost budget of 14,000, but incurred 1500 on couriers.

Work out:
1 the budgeted overheads and net profit margin percentage;
2 the effect of the couriers' bills on the overheads;
3 the effect of the increased overheads on the net profit margin percentage.

Even if you had trouble doing the arithmetic, you can see the disastrous effect that shoving unexpected costs into overheads can have. If the couriers' bills had been applied to the direct costs, the net profit margin would also have dropped, but it would have been noticed as soon as Project A was finished, when estimated and actual expenditures were compared. Then managers could have taken steps to curb this type of expenditure on other projects and maintained their overheads at 38 per cent.

Mark-up

The mark-up is another financial guideline. It is a factor that accounts for the overheads and the acceptable net profit margin, and it can be used in two ways. As mentioned above, publishers often start by setting the price they think the market will bear for a specific item. Dividing the proposed RSP by the mark-up shows the acceptable unit cost – the cost of producing each copy. With this goal in mind, the commissioning editor might then estimate the direct costs.

Working another way, the editor can divide the estimated direct costs by the proposed print run and multiply the result by the mark-up to show the RSP needed to make the acceptable margin. If the RSP is too high, the commissioning editor might have to revise the specification and costs, see how other income will affect the unit cost, or see if the mark-up can be varied for this project.

Exercise 2.4: Calculating unit costs and margins

Images & Ideas operates on a x6 mark-up, sells at a 25 per cent home discount to the trade and a 50 per cent export discount, and aims at a minimum 30 per cent net profit margin. Jan, a commissioning editor, wants to produce an illustrated book. She knows that the RSP should be no more than 20. Her first estimates of direct costs are 73,000 and overheads are calculated as 40 per cent of turnover. The sales manager has looked at the idea and said the maximum print run he would support is 15,000: 12,000 home and the rest export.

1   What is the unit cost Jan is aiming at?
2   Work out the unit cost and RSP Jan would achieve on the present estimates to see if she has attained her goal.
3   Find out how close Jan is to achieving the desired net profit margin percentage: the ratio of the net profit margin to the total income.

Jan obviously has not achieved her goal, so what should she do next? She should start by seeing how much other income the project might earn and calculating the effect this would have on the net profit margin. Let's say, for example, that the rights department thought it could contribute 20,000. What happens to the net profit margin?

turnover	210,000
other income	+ 20,000
total income	230,000
direct costs	− 73,000
gross profit margin	157,000
overheads @ 40% of turnover	− 84,000
net profit margin	73,000

ratio of net profit to total income:
73,000 ÷ 230,000 = 31.7%

Now Jan's project will get financial approval. If there had been no other income or if it had been insufficient, Jan would have had to revise her project to bring down its direct costs without affecting its quality and, therefore, selling price. Too often this is done by reducing the money for editorial work to a point where the quality of work needed cannot be guaranteed. Obviously, this is counter-productive. The overall quality of the book and its marketable price, however, will not be dramatically affected if there are minor changes to the specifications, such as a small reduction in the number of colour illustrations. Design and production colleagues often can also suggest ways of reducing costs.

Keeping to the budget

Estimates may have to be revised more than once before the acceptable margin is reached and the project is approved. An approved estimate becomes the budget. Remember, whether you help to set it or only receive it, maintaining the budget is part of your job. Even when a publication is not for sale – for example, an in-house magazine or a company report – producing it within budget is important to the organization's cashflow and overall finances. There are four ways to maintain the budget:

1 Ensure that the budget is adequate for the project you have to manage.

2 Negotiate payments for work with external suppliers in line with the budgeted amounts.
3 Control the quality of the work throughout its progress.
4 Maintain the schedule.

Point 1 refers to the parts of the budget you control. Many project managers are asked to provide costings for the elements for which they will be responsible. Responding to the brief and checking that the budget will cover all the relevant expenses is essential. If you have not been involved in creating the budget, you need to check how much has been allocated to all the jobs for which you are directly responsible, and determine whether it is sufficient for the *quality* of work required.

Some products are intended to be of the highest quality, others are not, and the time and money allocated for their production and the price charged for them reflect this intention. Just as the production manager will take this information into account in deciding whether to use cheap or expensive paper and where to place the printing, you need to use it in deciding whether the text will be subject to thorough copy-editing or just the imposition of house style, the artwork will be merely adequate or also attractive and imaginative, the photos will be of average quality and the often-seen or high quality and the more unusual, and the index will be simple or complex.

Point 2 is simple. You should spend no more money than is allowed. To do this, you can negotiate fees instead of hourly rates, or hourly rates with a limit on the number of hours the work is expected to take, in both cases reserving a small amount for contingencies.

Point 3 means you need to ensure that you get the quality of work the project requires at each stage of production in order not to cause excess expenditure in later stages. For example, if a text is poorly edited and requires more house corrections than allowed in the estimate or an extra stage of proofs, you have exceeded the budget. If illustrations are not clearly marked for size and have to be rescanned, you have exceeded the budget.

Point 4, which shows a direct connection between time and money, relates partly to direct costs, partly to overheads and partly to income. First, if slippage in one stage of the project has to be compensated for in another, the later stage might cost more than planned. For example, if the editor is late in handing over materials, the typesetter might charge extra for producing proofs on time if it means working overtime or over a weekend; if slippage in the pre-press stages of a project is compensated for only by the printing being moved from an inexpensive printer who cannot cope with the shorter schedule to a more expensive one who can, the direct costs for that part of the job will be exceeded. You might not control the part of the budget affected, but you are responsible for the action that has to be taken and, therefore, for the effect.

Second, salaries, an overhead, are related to productivity: the company pays X in salaries and expects to get Y finished projects a year in return. If fewer projects are completed in that time, it means that the company is paying more for each of them. That means the overheads per project are higher than forecast.

Third, bear in mind that if the press date is kept only through in-house staff working overtime, the overheads also rise. People working late are using more of the basic resources, such as lighting and heating, than was planned. Obviously, if staff get paid overtime or get time off in lieu, that increases overheads too. And when people work overtime frequently, and therefore are tired, they make more mistakes and gradually work more slowly, both of which also lower productivity and increase overheads. What happens if overheads increase? Obviously, as we have seen, the net profit margin is reduced.

Last, but not least, if publication is delayed, sales may be lost. The projected income is lower but the costs are at least the same or higher, so, again, the net profit margin is lower too.

A reduced net profit margin can be a problem not merely for a particular project, but for an entire list if slippage is common in the company. The decrease in income might be noticed immediately but the increase in overheads will be realized only some time later, when the annual accounts are done. As a result, there will be an unexpected shortfall in profits, which means there would be less money to invest in new business. But publishers have to continue investing in new projects or they'll go out of business. They will not want to raise their prices, because that could have an adverse effect on sales. And they will not want to reduce the direct costs for new projects if it means reducing the quality, because that, too, will have an adverse effect on sales. Therefore, they will see how they can reduce overheads. Salaries are a significant part of overheads. Fewer staff with a larger workload (i.e., the workload of 'redundant' colleagues) means higher productivity and lower overheads, even if some of that work is freelanced.

3 Assessing projects

You need to have certain information about a project in order to plan how to manage it effectively. Project managers can become involved in a commissioned project at various stages: when the commissioning editor is planning it, while the author is writing, or after the author delivers the final material. Assessment is a thought process. First you have to determine the purpose of your assessment. You can assess a project to:

* determine the nature and extent of work it will need to bring it to fruition;
* confirm or adjust schedules and budgets;
* see whether the materials received conform to the commissioning editor's original plan;
* plan your resources.

Then, in each case you need to examine the information and material you have to see what they tell you about the project, and to ask yourself what other information or material you might need.

Synopsis and specifications

A commissioning editor may determine the subject matter and approach of a work, or may agree to an author's proposal. In either case that editor is responsible for identifying the intended market and for deciding the specifications of the finished work. The publication date and budget are agreed when the proposal for the project is accepted, often before the complete text is received.

Estimating time

At the earliest stage the commissioning editor might give you an Advance Information Sheet (AIS), which states the specifications, summarizes the content, and lists the major selling points and the sales markets, so that you can estimate the time needed for each task, and the associated costs. What are you looking for? The specifications should tell you the format, the number of words as well as the page extent for a printed product or the timing for an audio tape, and the number and type of illustrations, if any. This information can help you to estimate how long the editing, proofreading and indexing will take and what they might cost, and the time needed for other stages of production. The same information, plus the list of sales markets, can also help you to estimate the time and costs for obtaining and using illustrations. However, if the AIS is your only source of information, your estimates need to be generous, to allow for all the contingencies you think might arise. Previous products in a series can provide useful information, but remember that each one can have its own potential problems.

Exercise 3.1: Using assessment of specifications and synopsis as the basis for scheduling

Below are the specification and synopsis for *What A Race!* and the commissioning editor's memo. After assessing this information, respond to the editor's request, using the global scheduling form to show the time allocated to each pre-press activity.

Format	245 × 190 mm
Binding	hardback
Extent	144 pp
Words	60,000
Illustrations	120, of which up to 100 in colour

Synopsis
What A Race! presents vivid accounts of the greatest horse races of the last 50 years by Morgan Steed, one of racing's most respected reporters, well known for his ability to convey all the excitement of the action. Looking back over his long career, Steed picks 50 races he's seen at major tracks around the world that were fantastic for the drama of their running, for their finish, or for a spectacular individual performance. Striking photos enhance the stories and make this an ideal present for racing fans everywhere. This is the fourth book in the very successful *What A ...!* series of highly illustrated sports books by the best writers in their fields.

MEMO

1 April
From: Commissioning editor
To: Project manager

I want to squeeze this title into the current programme. I already have an annotated list of races from Morgan. He'll be able to give us a list of pictures on Monday, 17 April, and the complete text by 3 July. I've discussed the schedule with Art Pen in design and Dot Prinz in production, and they say they need two weeks to produce pages and we have to pass the revises for press by Monday, 4 September, to meet our ideal publication date in October. Please provide an editorial schedule based on these dates.

Although nobody commits to a detailed schedule at this stage, it is important to decide whether the timescale is feasible, to think about what factors affect it, and to consider what information you will need for the next stage of planning. On the model answer, the critical path has been calculated from the date of passing the revised proofs back to the text-in date, and the subsidiary paths have been scheduled to coincide with the deadlines relevant to them.

Did you remember to schedule the jacket? This title has a short schedule, so it's important to produce the jacket quickly so that it can be used to promote sales. Notice that the arrow shows that work on the jacket can begin even before the picture list is in. In fact, because there is a series style to follow, the jacket can be briefed as soon as the decision to publish is taken. The synopsis and annotated list of races provide the basis for the blurb. Think what else you need to complete the brief: check that the author can provide suggestions for jacket illustrations, a biographical sketch and a photo of himself immediately. Scheduling the jacket should also prompt you to find out whether you will be expected to provide other sales material and, if so, what and when.

Drawing conclusions

All the photos will be sourced and the picture research can begin as soon as the list is in. Ask yourself if there is enough time to complete the research and selection before the text goes for setting. The synopsis tells you that the subject matter is tightly focused – horse races – so the like-lihood is that the majority of the images can be found in a few agencies specializing in sports, which is both time- and cost-efficient. There is plenty of time to get images from abroad, too, if local agencies can't supply them, and even to get one or two replacements if the author has to substitute a recent race in the final text. Once again, the advantage of this book being in a series means that if the pictures are available early, the pages can be designed by the time the text is ready for setting.

What else might affect the schedule? Check whether the author will be able to help with the picture selection and write the captions before the text is complete, without endangering the text-due date. Indeed, if the author is still writing his regular newspaper column, can you be sure that he will deliver the picture list and text on time? (See Chapter 4 for how to manage such situations.)

You should be able to deduce that this is a coffee-table book, and, therefore, there are not likely to be notes, cross-references or tables. While there is no perfect measurement for copy-editing time, because there are so many variables, it would be fair to say that a competent copy-editor would, on average, be able to copy-edit 2000 words an hour of well-written text uncomplicated by notes, tables, and refer-ences. Therefore, one week to edit these 60,000 words would be enough if the copy-editor were doing nothing else, especially as the text will be divided into 50 short, self-contained chapters, which means there will probably be few, if any, problems with consistency of information. Nonetheless, you must allow time for the author to respond to queries. And what if the editor has other work to do, or if the text is not as good as expected or is delivered on hard copy only, or the e-file is not worth using? Editing might take longer. Planning for such necessities and contingencies means allowing longer than the absolute minimum time, but not so long that the job is slowed down unnecessarily. Thinking about these issues should also lead you to plan to get some draft chapters to assess before the final text is due.

On average, a competent proofreader can correct eight to ten pages of straight text (i.e., no equations, formulas, notes, cross-references or illustrations) an hour. Therefore one week is enough time to proofread this book if the proofreader is working uninterrupted; two weeks allows for the fact the proofreader will have other work, as well as for interruptions and other contingencies. But what about the author? First, you need to find out how much time he has been given in his contract; two weeks is usually the minimum. If that's the case, you need to check that he will be willing and able to return his proofs a couple of days earlier than that, to allow his corrections to be collated with the proofreader's.

Again, on average, a competent indexer can create a simple index for a simple book at the rate of eight to ten pages an hour; factor in extra time for a more complex book or a more complex index. Then allow extra time for the indexer's other work, interruptions and contingencies. Compiling an index for this book in two weeks should be easy: the number of words and the limited range of the subject matter indicate a fairly short, simple index. To confirm your assessment, plan to check with the designer how many pages will be allocated to the index and, later, to discuss the brief with the indexer.

Some publishers allow or require their authors to provide the index to their books. This is fine if the author is an experienced and, preferably, trained indexer, but a possible disaster otherwise. The untrained author will take longer than a professional and the result might be so poor that it will adversely affect the quality of the book. Sometimes these authors prefer to pay for a professional indexer than to ruin their books. As project manager, you should check authors' contracts to see who is responsible for the index and whether authors have been sent any guidelines for producing one. You can also help authors assess their ability to create an adequate index, and advise them on the costs and benefits of employing a professional.

It will take little time for you to edit this index, and it can be set quickly, too. Even though there is a public holiday that week, there is sufficient time to check the corrections to the text proofs and to read the index proof, and pass both for press.

Remember that at each stage of the schedule you should allow time for:

- delivery of any materials that cannot be sent electronically;
- checking the quality of the material or work that has been done;
- preparing a brief to accompany the materials to the next stage;
- contingencies.

Draft text

There are three reasons to get drafts of a few early chapters before the entire text is due:

1 to find out what effect its format or quality might have on the schedule;
2 to see whether the author needs help to produce the agreed text on time;
3 to help you plan your resources.

Presentation

The way in which text and other materials are prepared can have an impact on the schedule, the budget and the production route. On hard copy all of the following slow down editing and typesetting:

* anything less than double spacing
* small margins
* faint print
* small typesize
* poor typing, noticeable in unwanted capitals, poor spacing, inconsistent styling
* illegible handwritten alterations
* additional text on small pieces of paper stapled or paper-clipped to another page

If the author provides only hard copy and it suffers from these problems, you need to allow more time in the schedule for editing, setting and proofreading. Most authors now provide their text electronically, and all but the last two problems can be overcome by reformatting the e-files and printing them out again. The cost of doing this is more than compensated for by the savings in time taken to edit and set. The last two problems require time to resolve even if the text is well presented in other ways.

For books or other documents with thousands of words, it is more efficient for copy-editors to work on hard copy first than directly on-screen, even if they will be inputting the changes to the files themselves. Unless editors have a desk-size screen, they cannot quickly and easily compare material in different parts of the text. Working through hard copy, editors can compile lists of global changes and manual search-and-replaces, thus moving quickly through the text and enabling the keyboarder to do the same.

If you print out the hard copy from e-files, you know it will be the author's final version of the text. When authors provide the hard copy with their files, you must check that the two match. First, ask authors if they have made any changes to the files after printing out; it is very tempting to do that, and many authors forget or are disinclined to produce a new printout. Then, because some authors may even forget that they have altered the e-file, run a check yourself: compare random pages of text and, particularly, tables, figures and references. A lot of time, and therefore money, will be wasted if an outdated version of the text is edited.

Most publishers brief their authors on how to prepare e-files. Usually, the main messages are just to type, not design, and to put notes, tables and figures in separate files. When authors justify text or use a lot of formatting – centring, tabs, different typefaces, sizes and attributes – it has to be stripped out before the files can be used for typesetting.

Exercise 3.2: Assessing presentation

The author has sent the following copy as an e-mail attachment labelled 'more text'. Assess the presentation only and list all your deductions. Then write a list of points that you will want to be conveyed to the author.

```
HEALTHY EATING
Health is always in the news.  At different times
throughout modern history we have been warned that eating
the wrong foods can be responsible for a host of
ailments, from acne to migraines, from cancer to stroke,
and so we are told what we should eat and what we should
avoid.  Unfortunately, although the experts agree on some
core foods in each list, there is often dispute about
others, or they move from one list to another as
scientific theory or knowledge changes.  And then theirs
the debate about whether organic food tastes better and
is better for you, or whether it is just more expensive.
With all the conflicting advice, it's no wonder that
people can get bored or confused.
```

THE RIGHT WEIGHT

The emphasis on being thin that was once focused only on women is now addressed to men too. On the one hand the mass media is full of images of super thin celebrities (photos) and on the other health experts write articles on the dangers of eating disorders and on being the right weight. But what is the right weight? There's obviously no *ideal* weight that applies to everyone, because we're all different shapes and sizes (photos of healthy people of different shapes and sizes). Instead of thinking of a specific ideal weight, we should think about a healthy weight range. And there are ways to tell what weight range is considered healthy for your size.

SIMPLE MATHS

Body Mass Index (BMI) is a tool used by health professionals to determine how healthy a person's weight is, but you don't have to be a doctor or a nurse to work it out. Here's how to find your BMI:

Weight in kilograms
Height in metres ^{2}

The following table shows you how to interpret your BMI:

BMI	Verdict
Up to 18	underwieght
18-24	normal
25-29	Overweight
30-34	Obese
35-39	Very obese
40 and above	extremely obese

As BMIs go up above the 'normal' range, so does the risk of high blood pressure and increased cholesterol levels. These conditions can cause heart disease and lead to strokes and other ailments (*see* pages xx).

SHAPE MATTERS

Even if your BMI is in the normal range, the shape your in could be unhealthy. If you have a large waist measurement and your shaped more like an apple than a pear there's an increased risk of diabetes, heart disease and other such ailments (photos of apple- and pear-shaped people).   The bigger you are around your waist proportionate to the rest of your body, the greater your risk of developing things like diabetes and some cancers. This increased risk is not because of the eight itself but because of where it is.

Men are more likely to be aware of there changing shape because trousers are sized by waist measurement. Women's clothing is sized differently, and the same size item by different manufacturers can vary greatly, so it is easier for them not to notice the extra inches. Even when people do notice, there is no guarantee that they will take action. Often as they age, people simply accept their changing shape as a factor of getting older. For your health's sake, its important not to let your body slide into an unhealthy shape.

Check your waist measurement by putting a tape measure around your waist just above your navel. (Can we have a drawing or a photo of how to measure waist?) Make sure the tape is secure but not tight. If you are a man and your waist is more than 94 centimetres, your health could be at risk; if it is more than 100 cm, it is at risk. Similarly, if you are a woman and your waist measure more than 88 cm, your health could be at risk but if its more than 88 cm it is at risk.* In all these cases, losing weight will make a difference.

A HEALTHY WEIGHT RANGE

The best weight for any individual is not a single number on the scales, and the problem of thinking of it this way is that it always keeps you just one kilo away from failure. To overcome this problem, it is better to think of your healthy weight as a range. This takes into account your body's natural fluctuations. The table below shows recommended target weight ranges for various heights and is intended only as a guideline; there are other factors that can affect the weight range that is most appropriate for you.

Target weight ranges

Height (m)	Weight (kg)
1.5	45–56
1.52	46–58
1.54	47–59
1.56	49–61
1.58	50–62
1.6	51–64
1.62	53–66
1.64	54–67

1.66	55-69
1.68	55-69
1.70	58-72
1.72	59-74
1.74	61-76
1.76	62-77
1.78	63-79
1.8	65-81

Healthy weight loss

Bookshop shelves are filled with diet books, each offering a slightly or even radically different way to shed unwanted pounds. And if that isn't enough, the pages of newspapers and magazines contribute at regular occasions: lose weight for summer, lose weight before the holiday feasting, lose weight *after* the holiday feasting, and so on. When you analyse them, no matter what the premise on which their based, the underlying factor is to eat fewer calories than you utilize. And naturally that is what this book recommends.

There are two ways to eat fewer calories than you use: cut down on the amount of food you eat, particularly of fats and sugars, and exercise more (perhaps we could have photos of people, adults and children, eating a small, healthy meal, playing various sports). You can do one or the other, or both. Just don't do it too quickly. The only way to lose weight and maintain the loss is to do it gradually. And the only way to do it and sty healthy is to eat a balanced diet.

A balanced diet

We are all used to being told to eat more fruit and vegetables. It is more helpful to understand how much of all types of foods to eat. Health experts divide food

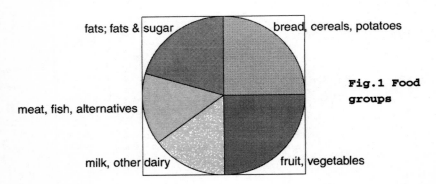

fats; fats & sugar   bread, cereals, potatoes

meat, fish, alternatives

milk, other dairy   fruit, vegetables

Fig.1 Food groups

```
into five groups.  The illustration below shows the
proportion of foods from each group that we should eat to
maintain a healthy, balanced diet.


In specific terms this means we should eat:
●  five or more servings of bread, cereals or potatoes
●  five or more servings of fruit and vegetables
●  three servings of milk or other dairy products
●  three servings of meat, fish and alternatives
●  two servings of food containing fats and two of
   foods containing fats and sugar
```

Notice that not everything you can deduce from the sample is negative or needs to be conveyed to the author. Although you don't want justified text and double spaces after punctuation, it is a simple matter to switch this formatting when you have the files. However, whereas it is also easy to make all the text and headings the same size and face, it might save the author time to type like that rather than format headings in different styles, unless, of course, you have provided a template. In most word-processing programs headings can be reformatted to 'sentence case', but this ignores proper nouns and changes *all* initial caps after the first word to lower case. It will save time and work to remind the author to capitalize words in headings only where grammar demands.

You need to consider the type size. In this example the small type-size and the single-line spacing make it impossible for a copy-editor to work on efficiently. If the author would be providing hard copy, you would want to tell him or her to increase the size to at least 10 point and to double space the lines. If the author would not be providing the hard copy, there would be no need to comment on type size or line spacing, as the files could be reformatted in-house before printing out.

What about the italics? Italics and bold do not *always* transfer from one software program to another. Ask whoever will be in charge of typesetting – the design or production manager – to check the file for compatibility generally and for these attributes particularly. Discuss with that person what should be done to overcome incompatibility; sometimes the most economical solution is to rekey all or specific elements of the text.

It is important to get the authors to make separate files for notes, tables, figures and photo suggestions; it's time-consuming, and therefore costly, to get the copy-editor to reorganize the files. For the same reason, you should also ask authors to number the tables and figures and refer to them in the text by those numbers rather than by direction.

Before discussing presentation issues with the commissioning editor and deciding who should talk to the author, assess the content of the sample material too.

Following the brief

Prepare yourself for assessing the content of the draft material by rereading the synopsis, specifications and contract or any other brief agreed by the commissioning editor and author. For printed publications, look too at specimen page designs or existing books in the same series to see what elements are included. When you do not have necessary information or are unsure about its interpretation, ask the commissioning editor. The latter is responsible for checking that the text is about the agreed subject matter and approaches the subject in the agreed way or conforms to the series style (for example, looks at the subject in its entirety or focuses on certain aspects, objectively or from a particular point of view, superficially or in depth) and is of editable quality. These are the criteria for accepting the text for publication. If you suspect that the commissioning editor has not yet looked at the draft material, keep these points in mind as you do your assessment, and report any problems.

To assess the text for your own purposes, ask yourself the following questions as you read:

* Is there evidence of all agreed elements, such as illustrations, tables or notes, and no unexpected ones?
* Is source material adequately acknowledged?
* Assuming that, ideally, all the chapters should be roughly the same extent, are these early chapters about the right proportion of the entire work?
* Based on the proportion of the text you have, do you think the author will be able to complete the job by the scheduled due date?

If the answer to any of these questions is no, identify what is wrong and discuss ways of putting it right with the commissioning editor. These are matters that have to be dealt with by authors. Early assessment provides an opportunity to help them get back on the right track before they have done so much work that revising, increasing or cutting the text, or finding source notes would be extremely difficult and endanger the schedule. It also indicates whether they need to be reminded of the deadline and whether you need to warn the project team of a possible delay.

Organization and quality

Not all problems with the text are necessarily going to be resolved by authors. First ask these questions about the text:

* Is it well organized, moving from the beginning through the middle to the end of each topic?
* Is it well structured, with the appropriate number and levels of headings for the intended readership?
* Are the structural elements – such as epigraphs, tips and project work – used consistently in all chapters?
* Is the information at the right level for the intended audience?
* Is the text well written and interesting?

If the answer is no, in each case decide how serious the problem is and whether the author can, or is the best person to, deal with it. Would any of these issues, for example, be handled more efficiently by the copy-editor, and what are the cost implications? Again, you will need to discuss your conclusions with the commissioning editor.

Complexity

The complexity of the work affects the schedule and can help you decide what skills or experience the copy-editor must have. Straight text is the easiest and quickest to handle in all stages of production. It takes more time to deal with additional elements, such as tables, notes, cross-references and illustrations. Tables, in particular, and illustrations can take a lot of time in design and typesetting. Look carefully at the examples of these elements in draft chapters:

* Do they relate well to the text?
* Are they accurate?
* Is the style consistent?
* Do they indicate that permissions need to be cleared?

Exercise 3.3: Assessing content

The text in Exercise 3.2 is roughly 10 per cent of one of the 10 chapters from a book to be titled *Here's to Your Health!* Using the AIS below, assess that text to answer the following questions, giving your reasons. Whenever an answer is no, suggest what can be done to rectify it.

- Is it about the agreed subject matter?
- Is it written from the agreed angle?
- Is there evidence of all agreed elements, and no unexpected ones?
- Is source material adequately acknowledged and will permissions need to be cleared?
- Is the draft text about the right proportion of the entire work?
- Is it well organized?
- Is it well structured, with the appropriate number and levels of headings for the intended readership?
- Is the information at the right level for the audience?
- Is the text well written and interesting?
- Do tables, figures, notes relate well to the text?

ADVANCE INFORMATION

ISBN	978-0-123-45678-X
Title	Here's to Your Health!
Author(s)	Dr Jackson Spratt, Dr Helen Cooke, and Alex Ciser
Affiliations	Dr Spratt writes weekly column in popular newspaper; Dr Cooke has weekly radio programme and writes column for popular magazine; Mr Ciser owns Ciser's Gym and is personal trainer to celebrities
Format	256 × 170 mm
Binding	Cased
Extent	304 pp, 125,000 words
Print run	25,000
Illustrations	75 colour a/w, 300 colour half-tones
Endmatter	Index
RSP	18.00
Publication	October next year

Rights sold   UK, Aus&NZ, USA, South Africa, France, Italy;
others available

Short description
Here's to Your Health! is a clear, no-nonsense approach to health
and well-being. Based on the latest accepted medical and scientific
knowledge, the simply written text dismisses dieting myths and fads
and promotes sensible and sustainable plans for the entire family.
Essential background information on how the body works and an
easy-to-follow explanation of a well-balanced diet are accompanied
by lively, full-colour diagrams. Full-colour photos illustrate the variety
of easy exercises, recipes and menus to suit different ages and
preferences. Questionnaires, tests and answers throughout the
book enable readers to evaluate their current lifestyle, while the text
motivates them to choose an appropriate programme to achieve
and maintain good health and well-being.

Selling points
- Authors are well known to the public as experts in their fields.
- Variety of exercises and menus to suit different lifestyles.
- Step-by-step illustrations for all exercises.
- 40 illustrated recipes.

As well as answering the specific questions in the exercise, did you
think about the photo suggestions? Although they need to be ex-
tracted from the text and might not all be used, they are at least
relevant. In such cases you also need to consider whether – and if so,
how – photos need to be referred to in the text. Figures can be used as
the basis for artwork and you could be thinking about briefing the
copy-editor to make such plain diagrams more interesting.

You should also have noticed that there are three authors. While
doing the exercise you could only wonder which author wrote this
draft and whether the others will be of the same quality; in reality,
you would make sure you had samples from all contributors. In
books with a large number of contributors each writing one or more
chapters or articles, it is usual to appoint a general editor, whose job
it is to coordinate and scrutinize the work of all the contributors so
that it arrives on time and fulfils the brief. In such cases the project

manager liaises with the general editor rather than with all the individual contributors.

In this project you would also want to find out if the other two authors are working in the same version of the same software as the one who has provided the sample. If they are not, check with the design or production manager to determine the best course of action. The more authors there are, the less likely it is that they will all be working in exactly the same software. You might have to assess the situation to see whether it would be best to convert all the files to one program, work on-screen with the files that are in the same program, or rekey some or all of the text.

Assessment of draft chapters can also help you decide the level of editing the text is likely to need:

* Minimum edit: imposing house style, dealing with inconsistencies and infelicities, few queries, marking-up for production.
* Medium edit: as above, but a moderate number of queries and limited reorganizing, rewriting, cutting or expanding.
* Major edit: as above, but many queries and extensive reorganizing, rewriting, cutting or expanding.

The heavier the edit, the more time it will take. The level of edit can also affect how useful the e-file will be for production. A minimum edit presents no problems: the editorial changes can be made economically by the copy-editor or the typesetter, although you should decide which one before the project begins. Similarly, a medium edit where the revisions are limited to chunks of text can still be done economically using the author's files. However, when an edit results in lots of small, unique changes throughout the text, it can be faster for a typesetter to rekey than for anyone to input just the changes. Whether major rewrites are best done on-screen by a copy-editor or on hard copy for a typesetter to key will depend on the copy-editor's computer speed and skills. Consult design and production to decide whether changes need to be made to the planned production route and to see how they might affect the schedule and budget.

Final delivery

Examining draft chapters is a rehearsal for assessing the entire job, although sometimes project managers are not involved before the final text is delivered. In either case, the first thing to check is that the material delivered is complete. If it is not, you need to identify what is missing, find out when it will be supplied, and decide whether work can begin without it. For example, a missing bibliography does not need to delay work on a book that has no references, but will delay or create extra work on one that does. A missing illustrations list may not need to delay editing, but it can cause delays in production if artwork or photos are not available when the text is ready to be set.

Next, check the length of the text. If it is only a small amount – say, 10 per cent – under or over the stipulated number of words, the copy-editor can be briefed to rectify it. However, when the discrepancy is greater, it needs to be discussed with the commissioning editor. Although generally it is unlikely that a deviation from the contract will be accepted, which would require the estimates to be revised, there are times when it is appropriate. Otherwise, the text needs to be returned to the author as quickly as possible: only authors should add or delete large chunks of copy, and they can do it best while the entire work is still fresh in their mind.

At the same time you should check that the agreed number of illustration suggestions has been supplied. If it has not, decide whether it is better to ask the author to rectify that now or to brief the copy-editor to do so in liaison with the author. In each case consider whether:

* the author is revising the text, and working on the illustrations will delay that work;
* the illustrations are so integrated with the text that only the author can provide the information for them;
* the author or the copy-editor is visually more able;
* not having the list with the text will cause scheduling problems at any stage.

See whether any changes that you or the commissioning editor requested after assessing the draft material have been done. If no changes were requested, look through the final text to confirm your initial assessment. If you did not have draft material, assess content and presentation as explained above.

4 Managing resources

Bringing a publishing project to fruition requires the combined efforts of editorial, design and production personnel. The nature of the project determines the specific composition of the team. In addition to the author, all books need a copy-editor, a proofreader, a designer, a production manager, typesetter and printer. Some publishers – mainly academic and STM (scientific, technical and medical) – require authors to provide all illustrations, to clear textual permissions and even to provide the index, but educational publishers and general trade publishers employ skilled professionals for these jobs. However, even academic and STM publishers employ indexers on multi-author publications. The team for an illustrated book might include a picture researcher, an illustrator or a photographer, or some combination of the three, as well as an indexer. Depending on the subject, commissioned photography might also require the services of other specialists, such as stylists or food technicians. In-house copy-editors often clear textual permissions, but some houses have a permissions department and others use freelance specialists for this task; freelance copy-editors can be asked to clear permissions but it is not automatically part of their job.

Figure 4.1 shows the most common project team members for books. For some projects there might also be consultants, reviewers or committees who see and comment on the work at particular stages. For projects that include multimedia components, the team might include actors, recording studio personnel, and webmasters.

Who does what?

The project manager selects, briefs and supervises the editorial team – copy-editor, proofreader, indexer and picture researcher – and is the main contact with the author throughout the project. In some types of publishing, particularly children's and educational, and in some houses the project manager is responsible for choosing the illustrator. In other cases the project manager briefs the design manager on what kind of illustrator is needed, the copy-editor prepares the specific

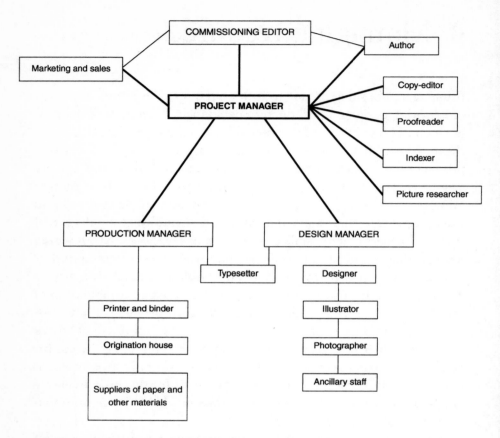

Figure 4.1 Potential project team members; heavy lines show project manager's direct contacts

illustration briefs, and the design manager chooses and contracts the illustrator and supervises the technical aspects of the work. Similarly, the project manager or copy-editor will prepare briefs for commissioned photographs, but the design manager or picture researcher will choose and supervise the photographer and ancillary staff.

A designer might do the typesetting. Otherwise, the production manager chooses and liaises with a typesetter, as well as the printer and binder, the origination house (if separate from the typesetter or printer), and suppliers of materials.

For the project to be successful, the editorial project manager must initiate and retain good communications not only with the members of the editorial team but also with the design and production managers. In some cases, project managers deal directly with freelance designers, and with typesetters and printers.

Choosing appropriate people

As soon as a project is fully conceived and the AIS prepared, it is easy to see what jobs need to be done. Look back at Exercises 1.3, 3.1 and 3.3, for example. In addition to a copy-editor and a proofreader, the basic information indicates whether the titles require an indexer, illustrator, or picture researcher. Choosing the most appropriate individual for each of these jobs can affect the quality, schedule and budget, and thus make the difference between success and failure.

Obviously, everyone must be competent in the basic skills required by their job. In Britain the National Occupational Standards in Publishing, which have been developed in consultation with the publishing industry, are the benchmark of competence for particular jobs, including editing and proofreading, commissioning and acquisition, and editorial management. The national origin is not important: the standards would be the same in principle everywhere. They break down jobs into their component elements and state what individuals must be able to do and what they need to know in order to do it. You can download these standards for free (see page 176). Use them to help you select team members – and be sure to read those for editorial project managers.

Competence is like the foundation of a building. After seeing that it is sound, you have to look at what is built on it to see whether or to what extent it suits your purpose. Many people have more than the basic skills to offer, and everyone has strengths and weaknesses. While reliability is another essential quality, you have to recognize that some people work more quickly than others. Similarly, you want all the team members to be good communicators, but some people will take more initiative than others in communicating. Because you have to balance the intended quality of each project with the time and money allocated for its production, assessing the project materials helps you to determine the specific skills and qualities each team member will need.

Copy-editors

Read the synopsis, advance information and, if you have it, sample text to help you decide what kind of copy-editor the project requires:

* a generalist, who works across a wide range of subjects for the general market;
* an area specialist, who works across a wide range of subjects in, for example, children's, educational or STM publishing;
* a subject specialist, one who has extensive experience, training or an academic qualification in the subject.

For example, a generalist would be appropriate for a biography of a scientist, an area specialist for a primary schoolbook on a particular science or combined sciences, and a subject specialist for a higher level textbook on a specific science. Many copy-editors are generalists who also specialize in particular areas or subjects.

As well as the type, consider the basic skills and qualities needed. Although they must be competent in what they do, not all copy-editors work with references or tables, for example. In qualitative terms copy-editors can range from only competent to brilliant in the skills that they do have; some, for instance, are better than others at raising queries, judging when to bend grammatical rules, restructuring text or dealing with stylistic infelicities. When you assess the text, you will see what basic skills the copy-editor must have and whether or not competence is sufficient.

Next, decide whether the project requires someone with additional skills, such as:

* altering the level of language;
* creating good artwork or photo briefs;
* reformatting text as tables, figures or other illustrations;
* working with notes and references;
* working with complex structures;
* restructuring or rewriting;
* working in particular computer programs;
* editing for multimedia use.

Exercise 4.1: Choosing an appropriate copy-editor

Look again at Exercises 3.2 and 3.3, and reread the relevant text. In one column list the aspects of the project that indicate particular skills or qualities the copy-editor must have, and in the next list those skills. For example:

Text	Skill
Minor spelling, syntax, consistency problems	Competent in basic skills
Wrong level for target market	Altering language level

The text is generally well written and at the right level, so the copy-editor does not need to be especially skilled at rewriting, and although the author seems slightly confused about heading levels, sorting them out is a basic skill. The draft material revealed some incomplete information; you need a copy-editor who will spot and deal with other such instances in the text. He or she needs to be competent at tables and be prepared to clear permissions when necessary. A competent copy-editor can edit and mark-up figures; someone who is visually adept can improve the way the information is presented. Similarly, any copy-editor should be able to convert basic metric and imperial measurements, but some people are better than others at understanding what level of precision is required in particular cases.

Did you realize the implications of multiple authorship? The commissioning editor should indicate whether the individual voices are to be retained or blended, and then you'll know which skill is required. In either case, the copy-editor has to be good at understanding stylistic differences. When a number of authors are contributing different chapters to the same book, the copy-editor has to ensure that the editing does not cause delays or instigate conflicts in the text or between the authors; this requires planning and good organization.

Proofreaders

Because their job is to provide an editorial failsafe (to catch editorial errors and omissions, and to query inconsistencies and ambiguities) as well as to correct literals, styling errors, misplaced text or illustrations and other elements of the typesetter's work, proofreaders can be categorized in the same way as copy-editors: generalist, area specialist, and subject specialist. Proofreaders have strengths and weaknesses too; for example, some are better than others at raising queries, judging which editorial changes are essential or desirable, or handling complex material.

Sometimes your choice of proofreader can be influenced by your choice of copy-editor as well as by the type of material. For example, if the copy-editor is chosen for his or her ability to rewrite text or to handle equations but is known to be weak on maintaining consistency of spelling or mechanical style, then you would want a proofreader with strengths to counterbalance those weaknesses.

Indexers

Always remember: a good index enhances a book; a bad index can ruin it (see page 37). Creating an index requires more than computer software: it is a skilled job, whose practitioners should be trained. Because it is important to understand the concepts in a text in order to select and cross-reference terms, indexers tend to be subject specialists. They might also specialize in media, indexing books, journals or web sites. Some are better than others, for example, in working on multi-author or multi-volume projects, in conceptualizing or in creating cross-references.

Exercise 4.2: Selecting a proofreader and an indexer

You need to select the other editorial members of the team to work on the book in Exercise 3.2. Using the information below, supplied by various colleagues, decide who you would use in each category, list the other two in order of preference, and give your reasons for choosing one and rejecting the others, for example:

Chosen:	Not chosen	Because
A		has skills x, y; quality z ...
	B	has skill x, but not quality z
	C	has ..., but not ...

Proofreaders
Harriet has a degree in business studies and worked in catering for a number of years before deciding to take a career break while her children are young. Always good at spotting spelling mistakes in

books and newspapers, she advertised her services as a proofreader and has been working for about a year, mainly on company brochures and reports. She is a friend of one of the authors.

After receiving a degree in history, *Tom* worked in the editorial department at Front & Back, a small general trade publisher, for two years, during which time he completed training courses in proofreading and copy-editing. He went freelance a year ago when Front & Back made him redundant, although it continued to use his services.

Dick trains nurses and other students in nutrition, and belongs to the college jogging club. He recently completed a proofreading course and has been getting steady work proofreading articles for health journals.

Indexers
Albert has a degree in chemistry and has been indexing for five years after completing a short training course. He has good computer skills and his preferred subjects include bio-medical research, chemistry, general medicine, nutrition and genetics.

Jack has a degree in chemistry and is an in-house copy-editor with five years' experience on a wide range of subjects at a popular level. He prepares indexes freelance. He has excellent computer skills and no subject preferences.

Zara has a degree in sociology and has been a proofreader for ten years. She completed a distance-learning course in indexing three years ago. She has adequate computer skills and her preferred subjects include personal development, popular medicine, food and drink, and mind, body and spirit.

Here's to Your Health! is a book for the popular market, so training and relevant experience in proofreading are more important than knowledge of the subject. Tom is an obvious first choice for these reasons. Dick is second choice because he doesn't have experience of proofreading books, which require more attention to consistency of style and content than shorter works. Although subject knowledge would be an advantage if Dick had the other qualities, journals tend to be at a higher academic level than popular books, so Dick might not be attuned to the type of queries to raise. Proofreading is much more than spotting spelling mistakes, so without relevant training Harriet is not a choice at all.

Zara is the first choice for indexer because she is trained and works in the subject area. Albert is trained too, but his preferred subject areas indicate a higher academic level. Although Jack has experience, there is no indication that he is a trained indexer or works in the subject area. The excellence of his computer skills is irrelevant on its own, and the fact that he has a full-time job means that not only is his time restricted, but also that the speed and quality of his indexing might be affected by his being tired after a day's or week's work.

Picture researchers

Picture researchers do more than just find photographs on a list; they negotiate the fees and clear permissions, prepare the acknowledgements and return photos to their sources, when necessary. They should pre-select photos so that you never see anything that is damaged or of poor reproductive quality, unless, of course, it is the only picture with the required editorial content. A good picture researcher looks for content and visual impact, and also pre-selects to provide the client with a reasonable choice rather than a large number of relatively similar items. Some picture researchers are better than others at pre-selection, finding photos that haven't been published before or often, seeing visual opportunities in the text in addition to those listed, finding special sources and negotiating fees. Internet and e-mail connections are essential to save time in communicating with sources that are not on the researcher's doorstep.

A generalist is appropriate for finding pictures on any subject whose sources are listed or whose content is broadly described; a specialist is better for locating photos when sources aren't specified or the content is more defined.

Some picture researchers also arrange and supervise commissioned photography; the briefs are provided by you or the copy-editor.

Exercise 4.3: Picking an appropriate picture researcher

Here are profiles of three picture researchers to consider hiring for *Here's to Your Health!*. As in Exercise 4.2, put them in order of preference, giving your reasons.

Picture researchers

Martha prefers to use e-mail to communicate with the client and to send the picture list to the widest range of sources, eliminating any photos that are not of good reproduction quality before sending the remainder to the client. She is efficient at preparing acknowledgements, returning any transparencies that have been used to their sources and handing over well-organized documentation at the end of the job, and finds that agreeing to the fees requested saves time. She always reminds clients when it is time to make a decision about transparencies so that they don't incur loan fees. Martha works on most arts and humanities subjects, and prefers not to get involved in selection meetings but to be given a list of gaps that need filling.

Melanie works for popular magazines as well as book publishers on a range of lifestyle topics, including health, fashion and beauty. She sends the picture list by e-mail to the sources she works with most often, requesting pictures she knows they have, and telephones and visits some of them herself. She pre-selects what she thinks are visually the best photos to bring to the client. Melanie is a good negotiator and prepares the acknowledgements and documentation adequately. She will attend meetings to try to ensure that her chosen pictures are selected, but will get other pictures if required.

Michael skims the text, adding suggestions and detail to the picture list. He will approach a wide range of sources by e-mail and a smaller group also by phone or in person, rejecting pictures with poor content or low reproductive quality before bringing the rest to the client. He asks to attend selection meetings and is good at filling gaps. He is adequate at negotiating fees, preparing acknowledgements and organizing documentation. Michael works on a range of arts and humanities subjects and specializes in sports, fitness and travel.

As a picture researcher, Michael contributes to the project by familiarizing himself with the material and suggesting additional pictures. He improves the chances of getting appropriate pictures by annotating the list, weeds out unusable pictures from a wide-based intake, saving his clients time, but doesn't limit their choice by imposing his own view of what is best. He's probably good at filling gaps because he involves himself in the selection meeting. Melanie knows her sources, but limits the client's choice by asking for known photos and then supplying only what she thinks is best. Picture researchers must have a good visual sense but should not try to impose their ideas on the client. Martha is organized but does not contribute to the project. Although she gets in the widest selection of photos, she makes no pre-selection for content or visual impact, leaving all the work to the client. She would be an appropriate choice when you need very specific subjects and have no budget concerns. All the picture researchers use e-mail, but Martha seems to use it to distance herself from sources and clients, whereas Michael and Melanie use it as only one means of research. Martha tries to ensure that the client doesn't pay loan fees when pictures are supplied as transparencies, but this is not a deciding factor: you could always tell other picture researchers to do this if necessary, and it is not necessary when sources supply digital images.

Selecting team members is, of course, not limited to reading profiles or a list of skills. You want to know about the quality of the work individuals do, whether they are quick or slow, can maintain schedules and budgets, and are good communicators. Discussing the possibility of a job with individuals – in effect, interviewing them – can provide some of the answers. People's views of themselves are not always objective or accurate, so getting opinions from colleagues or taking up references is useful too. You will form your own opinions when you supervise their work.

Finding freelancers

Copy-editors and picture researchers, like project managers, can be in-house or freelance; proofreaders and indexers are freelance. When you work in-house with copy-editors and picture researchers, your choice of team members may be limited, but you should still be aware of each person's skills and qualities so that you can manage the project in the most effective way.

When you work in-house and need to find freelancers for any of the editorial jobs, look at the files of freelance workers the organization has used before; these are most helpful if they indicate the projects worked on, the quality of the individual's work and his or her strengths and weaknesses, particularly with regard to maintaining schedules and budgets. If there are no files, ask colleagues, in your firm or elsewhere, for recommendations. If you are a freelance project manager, you might know other freelancers or sources for locating them. If none of the foregoing applies, look in relevant directories (see page 176). Make a list of apparently appropriate people to approach for each job.

Negotiating

After you have determined the type of people you need and how to find them, hiring them involves negotiating time and money. The amounts allocated will influence the quality of work to be expected. Remember, the publisher decides the intended quality level, from poor through mediocre to excellent, and your job is to know what that intention is and to ensure that the work for which you are responsible fulfils it.

Preparation

The first step is preparation. Make sure you know:
1 how many hours the work will take to complete;
2 how much time there is in the schedule;
3 how much money there is in the budget;
4 house and market rates for the job;
5 what expenses might arise.
Chapter 3 explained how to assess a project for scheduling on the basis of early information and draft material, so you know how to satisfy points 1 and 2. Work out the earliest and the latest starting date that will maintain the schedule and still incorporate some contingency time, so that you have room for negotiation. Always remember that you have to allow more time than the number of hours the work will take to do: most people, in-house or freelance, usually do not work exclusively on a single project, and even when they do, administrative tasks, meetings, e-mails, phone calls and other interruptions will occupy some of their available time.

If the publisher has hourly rates for the different jobs, they will be the basis of the commissioning editor's budget. For point 3, check how much the budget allows for each job in total and how many hours that is at the house rate. Next, point 4, compare the house rates to the market rates (see the web sites of the various freelance organizations for recommended rates) to see whether the former are high, low or average, which can indicate whether you will be able to afford the quality or worker you need. Compare the number of hours at these rates with your assessment of time for each job. Some jobs are done in stages, so be sure to take into account, for example, not only the hours the copy-editor works before the material goes for setting but also the time that might be spent later adjusting pages, collating the proofs, and so on. You should also be prepared to accept interim invoices if the work is spread over a long or broken period.

Some budgets show the fee for the job and allowable expenses separately. If your budget doesn't, point 5 tells you to think about what expenses might be incurred: travel to meetings or for research, postage, photocopying or telecommunications, for example. Take this figure into account before you work out the hours the fee will cover. Remember to make sure that the budget for picture research separates the researcher's fee from the cost of using the pictures.

Approach

Now that you have prepared yourself, you are ready to make initial contact. Freelance workers tend to book up weeks or months in advance, so approach people well before they will be needed. This gives you a reasonable chance of getting the person you want, and it allows you time to look for someone else if your first choice is unavailable and to take up references before the work begins.

When you do not know the person you are contacting, first introduce yourself and the company you represent, and ask whether it is convenient to talk – don't just assume; make this polite enquiry before beginning conversations even with people you know well. Explain how you acquired the person's name: from a colleague or in the company's file, from a credit in another book or from a directory or web site. Then, describe the project broadly – a text/an illustrated book/ catalogue/encyclopedia/teacher and student books about . . . – and confirm that the person does the relevant kind of work and in the subject area. Mention the extent and number of illustrations, and whether the work is to be done on hard copy only or also on-screen.

Outline the general schedule: expected starting date, and amount of time the job should take. Confirm the person's interest and availability before going into detail about the material or the schedule. When people are interested but can't start work on the given date, see if you can negotiate a date between the earliest and latest possible starting date. The closer to the latest date you get, the more certain you need to be of the individual's reliability. If the individual is still unavailable, ask whether he or she would like to suggest someone else. When the answer is yes, check whether you are being given contact information only or a recommendation.

When you have outlined the nature of the work, the level of edit, and the time you estimate it will take to complete the job, discuss the fee. Do not ask what the freelancer charges – that gives the freelancer control of the negotiation. Offer a fee. Start with an amount somewhat lower than the maximum available to allow room for bargaining, and keep a small amount in reserve for contingencies. Since you have already discussed how long you think the job will take, the freelancer can work out the hourly rate. Many freelancers prefer fees because it helps them to plan their cashflow.

Most freelancers will not commit to the schedule or the fee without seeing at least some of the material and a full brief. The more accurate your assessment and description of the material at this stage, the more likely it is that they will confirm both details when they have had time to assess the material themselves. However, you must always advise all team members, whether in-house or freelance, to tell you as soon as possible of any reason why they will need more time or money. That is why you schedule and budget for contingencies.

Exercise 4.4: Negotiating with freelancers

The budget for *Here's to Your Health!* includes:

copy-editing	2950
proofreading	670
indexing	610

The commissioning editor created the budget using the final costs of a project of the same specifications that was published six months ago. Looking through the file on that project, you see that the editor did the copy-editing, collated the proofs, and briefed the illustrator. The project manager undertook all other editorial tasks.

Estimates of time for the work to be done are:

copy-editing	130 hours
preparing a/w briefs	10 hours
checking a/w visuals	5 hours
proofreading	28 hours
collating	10 hours
indexing	30 hours

Claire is an excellent copy-editor on hard copy and on screen, experienced in this subject area, and visually creative. She usually asks 20.00 an hour to work on-screen.

Greg is a competent copy-editor, less experienced than Claire in all respects, but has good visual skills. He is willing to accept 18.50 an hour.

Tom, the first choice for proofreader, usually asks for 17 an hour, whereas *Dick* will accept 14.50.

Zara, the indexer, calculates her fees on the basis of 20.00 an hour.

Choose a copy-editor and proofreader, and say how you will allocate the work and the money to them, and how you will negotiate with the indexer. You must not go over budget. List the work you will do yourself.

The commissioning editor made two mistakes: not adding an amount to account for inflation over an eighteen-month period – a project published six months ago was probably budgeted and began work a year and a half ago – and not adding any contingency money to actual costs. For these reasons you don't have quite enough money to agree the preferred rates of your first-choice workers with a safety margin for unexpected problems or even an expenses allowance. You might have been tempted to choose Greg as the copy-editor because his asking price would bring the job in under budget. However, Claire is the best person for the job, and using her can assure you of the quality of work on text and artwork. As a result you are unlikely to have to undertake any remedial work yourself, which would add to overheads and could cause delays, and there should be minimal editorial corrections at proofreading, This, in turn, means that the budget for typesetting corrections will be maintained and that proofreading can be done in the time allowed, saving the contingency budget. Similarly, use Tom for the proofreading and collating because he is the best person for the job. A proofreader who is good at querying saves the editor's time by asking only necessary questions and in a clear, concise way.

The purpose of offering a lower figure than the budget contains is only to allow for expenses and contingencies, not to come in under budget. Therefore, the amount you aim to keep in reserve should be proportionate to the job: the greatest unknowns are in the text before it is edited, so its contingency budget is larger than that for the other two jobs.

In each case in the exercise, the fee offered represents only a small reduction of the individuals' preferred rates. If you offer a fee rather than an hourly rate, freelancers may calculate that they can work at a pace that provides them with an equivalent of their hourly rate, or better. However, if you offer much less than an individual's usual rates, that person might decline the job or explain that some aspect of the job might have to be sacrificed. Sometimes the work takes longer than expected and you should be prepared to adjust the fee – remember your contingency fund. However, be aware that some freelancers might be reluctant to ask for more money in case they are accused of being slow. The result will be either that they lose money on the deal, which is unfair, or rush through the job and not do it properly, which is not what you want. You can avoid these problems by asking appropriate questions when you are monitoring the schedule.

Rather than risk having to use someone without the necessary skills for the job or sacrificing some element, base the figures you contribute to the creation of a budget on the current market rates for the required level of quality, plus an amount for contingencies. When you have not been involved before the budget is agreed, analyse the amounts that have been allocated and discuss with the commissioning editor any problems that shortfalls will produce.

Styles of management

If you work in-house, an alternative answer to Exercise 4.4 is for you to collate the proofs yourself. Then you could afford to pay the others their going rate and still have a small general contingency fund. Collating the proofs yourself helps you to evaluate the work of the copy-editor, proofreader and typesetter. It does not take long and so would not affect the scedule or overheads.

How you organize the editorial team will depend on the extent to which you can or wish to delegate responsibility, the composition of the team, and your overall workload and budget. For example, if you were to choose the alternative answer to the last exercise, you would have to make sure that you had the time and budget to do the collation yourself. The style of management you choose may influence, or be influenced by, your choice of personnel.

After establishing the team and setting schedules, some project managers like to brief and have all the editorial team members communicate only with them. They liaise with the author over queries, with the picture researcher, with the author and design manager over artwork approval and picture selection, and with the production manager throughout manufacturing (Fig. 4.2). This gives project managers complete control of every stage of the job, but it takes a lot of their time and limits the number of projects they can manage

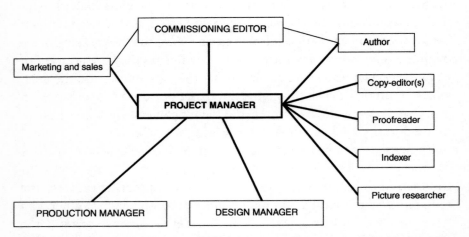

Figure 4.2 Project manager as sole link between all team members after work on text begins

simultaneously. Unless they are doing the copy-editing themselves or familiarize themselves with the text in detail, they will be at a disadvantage in dealing with authors' answers to editors' queries, proofreaders' queries, briefing the indexer and editing the index, briefing and approving artwork, and briefing and selecting photos.

When projects are so large or complex that more than one copy-editor is required, project managers must be deeply involved in the detail of the project and handle queries, illustrations and editing the index themselves.

Otherwise, project managers can delegate varying degrees of responsibility to copy-editors. They may, for example, ask copy-editors to work directly with authors on textual queries and to brief the indexer and edit the index; or also to work with the author, picture researcher and designer, as relevant, on artwork approval or picture briefing and selection (Fig. 4.3). Exercise 4.4 shows how this might work: checking the artist's visuals as well as preparing the artwork briefs is delegated to the copy-editor, which means the project manager can check and approve the final work by comparing it to the approved visuals, whereas the budget limitations make it necessary for the project manager to take complete control of picture research.

When project managers delegate the maximum number of tasks, they supervise the main stages of the work and attend handover and,

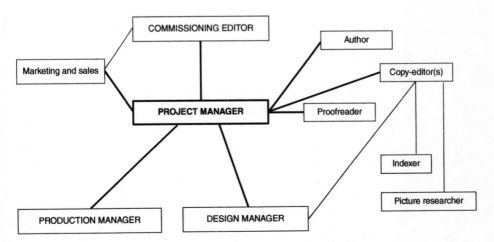

Figure 4.3 Project manager as central organizer, delegating some responsibility to the copy-editor

perhaps, illustrations meetings – be sure to annotate your scheduling form with these key dates – maintain direct contact with the proof-reader, the design manager or freelance designer, and the production manager or the typesetter and the printer, and remain the main contact for the author.

Managing a close relationship with authors is a very important part of the job. Remember that you are dealing with their 'baby'; authors like to, and should, feel that both they and their offspring are being looked after. Although the commissioning editor should be available to authors for guidance and support during the period of writing, project managers often get involved at this stage, sometimes assisting or substituting for the commissioning editor. Otherwise, their role at this stage should be to check that authors are working to schedule, preparing materials in the agreed way and according to the brief. When the material is delivered, the project manager must retain close contact with authors as the company's main representative, through all stages, again to ensure that the schedule is maintained, to preclude conflict by resolving any differences of opinion between authors and other team members, and to keep authors informed, involved and motivated.

5 Briefing

Briefs give people the essential information and instructions that enable them to do their jobs. There is always a degree of assumed knowledge, ranging from basic to specialized, so a brief contains information relevant only to a specific job. In the process of selecting the most appropriate people for the project, you are establishing that they have the knowledge and skills needed to interpret and carry out the brief.

The principles

The better the brief, the greater the likelihood that the job will be done as you want it, on time, within budget and to the specified quality. Briefing is both oral and written. Talking to team members helps you to establish the rapport and clear lines of communication that are essential to good project management. You can discuss the project as a whole, the author and the specific task, whereas in the written brief you will summarize essential points.

A good written brief is:

* complete
* concise
* clear
* consistent

Include all the information people need to produce the results you want, but no more, or you risk inhibiting their contribution or wasting their time. Also, when briefs are too long or complex to be assimilated or checked easily, some points might be forgotten or overlooked. Long briefs are as counterproductive as the term is paradoxical. Make sure the briefs you prepare are precise, unambiguous and not contradictory.

Follow up written briefs a few days after sending them to check whether the recipients understand the detail and have everything they need, or you need to answer questions or provide other information or materials. If you and the team members work in-house, it is easy to do this face to face, or if you are physically very distant from each other, by phone. Ideally, use the phone to check with team members when you and/or they are freelance. Speaking to people is quicker than exchanging a series of e-mails, and listening to someone can often tell you whether they really have understood specific parts of the brief or need clarification. Always remind your colleagues to contact you when they need to ask you for or give you information.

Creating the brief . . .

There are three sources of information for creating the brief:
1 The commissioning editor's brief to you
2 The contract, synopsis and AIS
3 Your assessment of the material
The better the brief you receive from the commissioning editor, the easier it will be for you to gather the information you need to pass on to others. However, not all commissioning editors give briefs, and the briefs that some give are inadequate. Therefore, your assessment of the material is always the most important basis for the brief.

In-house project managers should have access to the contract, but freelance ones don't. If you are freelance, you may need to ask for those contract details that can affect the schedule or general running of the project.

For authors

The commissioning editor's brief to authors concerns the content. Ideally, it has been summarized in writing and passed to you; this is not always the practice, though it should be, so you have to be prepared to work without it. Your brief to authors concerns the processes and the schedule. Particularly when the project is an author's first, outline what will happen to the material when it is delivered. Explain each stage briefly and give the author a general idea of the time allocated to it. The time allowed for authors to read their proofs is in their contracts, but should be repeated. This is a good opportunity to explain to or remind them that they can make only essential corrections, not changes, at proof. Proofs are not an opportunity for rewriting.

It is best to do the first briefing as soon as possible, and to do it orally, so you can immediately establish a relationship and respond to what authors already know and to their questions. Mention the name of anyone the authors will be in contact with and what the purpose of that contact will be, and establish the authors' availability. Follow up the oral briefing with a letter or e-mail confirming the names of the people and the dates discussed.

When you send the authors their proofs, tell them the date the proofs must be back in-house and remind them that only essential corrections – those that will affect the saleability of the book – should be made. Be sure to check your authors' contracts for any clause that covers proof corrections, since this may affect the issue.

Particularly in academic publishing, authors are sometimes required to provide their own artwork, in which case they should be briefed at the beginning of the project on how to present it. Although they may be dab hands at computer graphics, they might not know what is necessary for reproduction. Discuss the technical requirements – for example, software program, file types, colour palette, style, consistency, presentation of annotations – with the design or production manager and then with the author, and confirm the detail in writing. Artwork prepared by illustrators is discussed later.

For the entire editorial team

The starting point for a brief is the end-product. In order to tell people what you want them to do, you have to identify the desired results of their work. Although you need to create separate briefs for each job, some information is common to all, and most of it is found on the AIS:

* title
* author
* format: page size and binding style/web site/CD/audio tape
* extent: number of pages, duration of tape
* number of words
* number and types of illustrations
* use of colour
* summary of contents
* edition: new/revised/number
* series or volume: part of existing series/first in a series/individual
* publication date
* recommended retail selling price
* intended audience: age range, interest level and knowledge level

● market: domestic, specific foreign countries, or international
This part of the brief provides the context within which everyone works. In total, it establishes the general nature of the product and the market. In particular, the specifications of size and content relative to price give an idea of the quality level expected, previous editions or volumes in a series provide style guidance, and the publication date is the first indication of the schedule. Including an AIS as part of the brief helps you to keep the covering letter short. When you are adding new members of a team to a series or loose-leaf project, providing them with copies of existing materials serves this purpose.

For copy-editors

There are five elements to the brief for all copy-editors, and a sixth one for freelancers:
1 A list of the materials supplied
2 Relevant background
3 The level of the copy-editing task
4 A list of specific tasks or responsibilities
5 The schedule
6 The agreed fee
A handover form is an efficient way of dealing with point 1. Figure 5.1 shows an example of such a form, which can be used by commissioning editors to hand over the materials to you, and by you to hand over the materials to others. It can be sent with e-files or hard copy. It includes relevant information about the title and the names of team members who might work on or with these materials (other than the indexer, because he or she comes in at a later stage, when everything has been resolved), as well as a checklist on which you can quickly indicate what is being delivered with the form, what is to come and when, what is not relevant and, for prelims, what you want the copy-editor to originate. The form shown also provides a useful reminder for you to supply new freelance editors with a house style guide, and for all editors to attach the editorial style guide they create while they work, so that it can be handed on to the proofreader. Recipients should always be asked to check that they have received exactly the materials listed. Then when items are missing, they can be traced quickly, which improves the chances of finding them. If you send any items that are not listed on the form, such as sample designs

---

HANDOVER FORM

ISBN _____ Publication date _____

Title _____

Subtitle _____

Author(s)/editor(s)
translator(s)/compiler(s) _____

Format _____ mm, hb/pb _____ Extent _____

Commissioning Editor _____ Project Manager _____

Copy-editor _____ Proofreader _____

Designer _____ Picture Researcher _____

Indicate below which items are included with the edited test, and which are to come and <u>when</u>. Delete those that are inapplicable.

Text
- ❏ half-title_____
- ❏ half-title verso_____
- ❏ title_____
- ❏ title verso_____
- ❏ dedication_____
- ❏ epigraph_____
- ❏ contents list_____
- ❏ preface_____
- ❏ foreword_____
- ❏ acknowledgements_____
- ❏ © permissions_____
- ❏ list of contributors_____
- ❏ list of figures_____
- ❏ list of illustrations_____
- ❏ list of maps_____
- ❏ list of tables_____
- ❏ list of abbreviations_____
- ❏ other prelim matter?_____
- _____
- ❏ appendix(es) _____
- ❏ footnotes_____
- ❏ end of chapter notes_____
- ❏ end of text notes_____
- ❏ glossary_____
- ❏ bibliography_____
- ❏ further reading_____
- ❏ useful addresses_____
- ❏ other endmatter?_____
- _____

- ❏ Hard copy

- ❏ CDs/e-files
- No. enclosed/attached_____
- Format_____
- Software_____
- ❏ list of files attached
- ❏ list of files on printout
- ❏ key to codes in e-file
- ❏ key to codes on printout

Illustrations
- ❏ photos (indicate no.)_____
- integrated/section
- halftone _____ colour_____
- ❏ artwork: roughs/finished (indicate no.)
- line_____ tone_____
- b&w_____ 2-colour_____
- 3-colour_____ 4-colour_____
- ❏ maps: roughs/finished (indicate no.)_____
- ❏ captions_____
- ❏ annotation lists_____
- ❏ tables (indicate no.)_____

- ❏ **House style sheet**

- ❏ **Project style sheet**

- ❏ **Permissions letters**

Figure 5.1 A handover form, to be filled in by the commissioning editor and the project manager

or previous works in the series, you can add them to the form or list them in your letter.

Relevant background about the title that you would discuss with copy-editors might include:

* how the subject is being approached;
* changes that have been agreed with, or rejected by, the author;
* main problems with the text, including whether it needs cutting or expanding, and by how much;
* the proportion of space allocated to text and illustrations;
* how the title relates to a series or list;
* implications of the target audience and sales market.

Point 2 might also be relevant information about the author, such as particular sensitivities, availability, contact details and, in the case of multiple authors, whether to approach all of them or one appointed as the liaison. As always, the written brief should summarize the main points of your discussion.

In discussing point 3 you can clarify what you mean by a minimum, medium or major edit (see page 48), mentioning examples in the text and emphasizing any restrictions; in writing, you can reduce this to a one-line summary of the level, and bullet points, if necessary, for the restrictions.

You must make clear whether copy-editors are to work on hard copy or e-files or both (see page 38). Depending on how experienced a copy-editor is, you can discuss in more or less detail other tasks to be done, and summarize them in your briefing letter or on another checklist, such as the one in Figure 5.2.

Figure 5.3 shows an example of another form, which copy-editors complete for the benefit of designers and typesetters. It can be a separate e-document or the back of a printed handover form. Obviously, you can design forms that are relevant to your type of publishing.

Points 5 and 6 will have been discussed when you approached and negotiated with the freelance copy-editor; you need to confirm them in writing when you hand over the materials. When accepted by the other party, the letter and accompanying documents, such as the specifications, form a contract, so it is important to tell the copy-editor to let you know as soon as possible if there are any problems with time or money. If the copy-editor is in-house, you need to give him or her the schedule and a reminder to alert you to problems at any time.

COPY-EDITING CHECKLIST

Title:_____ Author:_____

Queries
- ❏ Resolve with author
- ❏ Send to project editor

Permissions
- ❏ Check
- ❏ Clear
- ❏ Prepare detailed list of items needing
- ❏ Check acknowledgements
- ❏ Write acknowlegements

On hard copy
- ❏ Edit and mark up
- ❏ Key in tables & illustrations
- ❏ Separate tables, figures, notes from text

On e-file
- ❏ Input editorial changes
- ❏ Tag and code for setting using QuarkXpress tags/colour/other
- ❏ Create separate files for tables/figures/captions/notes
- ❏ Format output as _____
- ❏ Cut and fill pages as required
- ❏ Collate proofs

Prepare briefs for
- ❏ Artwork
- ❏ Approve artwork visuals
- ❏ Approve final artwork
- ❏ Photography
- ❏ Picture research
- ❏ Index
- ❏ Check commissioned photos
- ❏ Select photos
- ❏ Edit index
- ❏ Edit captions
- ❏ Write captions

Liaise with
- ❏ Project manager only
- ❏ Designer
- ❏ Illustrator
- ❏ Picture researcher
- ❏ Indexer

Figure 5.2 A sample checklist to accompany the copy-editor's brief. You can modify it to reflect the nature of the projects on which you work.

NOTES FOR DESIGNER

Title: _____   Author: _____

Editor: supply MS folios in general. In the case of numerous headings, extracts, etc., cite the first few instances/longest and shortest, and point out any anomalies.

Running heads   recto _____
(attach list of shortened   verso _____
headings if necessary)   none _____

Section/part opener   _____

Chapters   _____

Subheads   A _____

                                          B _____

                                          C _____

                                          D _____

                                          other_____

Epigraphs   _____

Extracts   verse_____

                                          prose _____

                                          drama _____

                                          correspondence _____

Tabular matter
                                          _____
Display matter
                                          _____
Lists
                                          _____
Footnotes
                                          _____
Special sorts/symbols
                                          _____
Spaces in text
                                          _____
Other items
                                          _____

                                          _____

Special instructions
                                          _____

                                          _____

Figure 5.3 An example of a handover form, to be filled in by the copy-editor

Exercise 5.1: Briefing a copy-editor

In Chapter 4 you chose Claire to copy-edit *Here's to Your Health!* You discussed the project with her in November and she can begin work in mid-January. She will edit the text and write creative briefs for the artwork.

The pass-for-press date is 3 July. In response to your queries, the designer has said that the illustrator wants three weeks to produce visuals and another three weeks to produce final artwork, and that typesetting will take about four weeks. The jacket is finished.

Hard copy and e-files of the full text and all ancillary materials arrived on 11 January. The authors have followed your request to put tables and figures in separate files and to make a separate list of photo suggestions, but they have kept references to figures and photos in the text. They have also left the footnotes in the text. Looking through the full manuscript, you see that there appear to be a few items requiring copyright permissions. You will ask Claire to send you a list so that you can clear the permissions.

Review all the relevant material in Chapters 3 and 4. Use a global schedule form to work out a schedule for the critical paths for text, essential text-related activities that involve you or the copy-editor, and artwork, and prepare a written brief for Claire. In your letter, which can, of course, be an e-mail, indicate any other briefing materials that you are including or attaching.

However you worded the letter, it probably didn't present any difficulties, and including the AIS and handover form made it short and simple. Notice that Claire is asked to check the handover form against the materials received.

Because Claire will be inputting changes to the e-files, she needs to provide a clean printout of the final version. Even though most copy-editors find it efficient to work first on the hard copy of the text, particularly of complex books, before inputting changes, they will also do some work directly on-screen, such as global changes and final finessing. Looking through the original hard copy may give you an insight into how heavily the copy-editor has edited. As well as showing the mark-up, the new printout is a fail-safe back-up if anything were to happen to the e-files.

How did your schedule compare to the one suggested in the answer? Did you remember that the final artwork, ideally, had to be in and approved by the time the text went for setting? Using the information in the exercise, you should have worked out the relative periods of time for briefing and checking artwork. Your answer might not be exactly the same as the model; just make sure you have allowed a reasonable amount of time, including contingency time. Check with design and/or the illustrator that the time for each stage is adequate, too. Notice that on the model answer the amount of time for editing the text might be longer than strictly needed, but there is no point in rushing to set the text. Sending the illustrations with the text potentially reduces the number of proof stages.

There are two public holidays during the setting, and you would need to check with production that there would still be adequate time for the work to be done. If holidays occur on different dates on your answer, check that the time remaining is adequate for the nature of any work affected. The model answer extends the typeseetting period by a week to allow for the holidays and the designer's less than precise reply ('about four weeks').

There are only a few items that might need permissions, so the answer asks for the list soon, assuming it will not take Claire long to create it. You might have decided to give her more time because you think it will not take long to clear only a few items. However, sometimes a single item can take a very long time, so it is safest to allow the maximum time available. Of course, there are some, mainly academic, publishers who require their authors to clear their own permissions before submitting the final text. In such cases you need to get the documentation from the author to check that the permissions have been cleared for the appropriate markets and to ensure that the acknowledgements are worded correctly.

Claire is asked to return all other materials to you a few days before you need to send them to the next stage of production so that you have time to check the work, key in the photos and prepare the next brief. You might need only a few hours, but planning to have a few days allows for other work you might have to do and means that there is still adequate time if the materials arrive, say, a day later than requested. Reminding Claire to provide her style sheet and complete the notes for the designer makes your next brief easier.

Dr Spratt is named as the author contact. It would be all right if you had Claire contacting all three authors, but using one of a team of authors is a more efficient use of the copy-editor's time. It is essential to think about this at the beginning of a project and confirm the arrangement first with the commissioning editor and then with the authors.

Think of the different ways in which material can be sent – e-mail, regular post, special delivery, courier – and the project's needs; for example, are there any problems sending files by e-mail, are there materials that must be sent as hard copy, is the schedule so tight that you cannot wait for postal delivery, have you allowed for courier services in the budget? State how to return the materials so that you remain in control of the schedule and budget.

The letter mentions all the major tasks to be done (you might have used a form) and the fee, and reminds Claire to contact you if any problems arise. It also has a word of welcome. Phrase it as you like and put it at the beginning or the end, but do it: making people feel appreciated even before work begins helps the working relationship.

For designers and typesetters

For most printed publications, the page design has usually been agreed with the commissioning editor before the text and other materials are ready for production. After you have assessed the author's materials, review the design. Check that the following are adequate in size, clear, accessible and appropriate to the purpose of the publication and the level of readership:

* margins
* type faces, sizes and leading
* running heads and folios
* spacing between columns and between illustrations and text

Also make sure that:

* captions are allowed sufficient space;
* headings are clear and clearly differentiated;
* tables incorporate all necessary elements;
* figure references and internal cross-references have been styled;
* all editorial elements have been styled and are appropriate.

Your job is not to judge the design according to your aesthetic preferences but to ensure that it works for the material and the reader. When an aspect does not work, say why it doesn't and, if you can, what the solution might be. Be objective: always refer to the element, not the person. Say, for example, 'The side margins need to be about X mm wider to allow a child in this age range to hold the book without obscuring the text' rather than 'You've made the margins way too narrow.' Resolve all design and typographical issues before sending material into production.

Check the handover form and materials returned by copy-editors to make sure they are consistent and complete. When typesetters rather than copy-editors are inputting editorial changes to authors' e-files, attach the copy-editor's list of global changes to the handover form. Designers can use the form in Figure 5.2 as a guide in checking the mark-up, and revise any design specifications if necessary. When designers are not doing the typesetting, they will prepare the type specification and send it with the materials to the production department or typesetter. However, in format publishing and established loose-leaf projects, you will send the materials to typesetters working to an existing specification.

Your covering letter or memo should state what you are handing over and what kind of proofs you expect and when. As usual, you should ask to be notified as soon as any problem with the materials or schedule is noticed.

For proofreaders

The brief for proofreaders is similar to that for copy-editors:
1 A list of the materials supplied
2 Relevant background
3 The type of proofreading to be done
4 A list of specific tasks or responsibilities
5 The schedule
6 The agreed fee

The production route should have been established at the beginning of the project. If it wasn't, find out before you contact the proofreader whether proofs will be sent as hard copy or PDFs, and whether PDFs have been prepared as PaperlessProofs (see Glossary). The chosen route has an impact on the schedule and budget. When you are sending PDF proofs, you need to agree with the proofreader:
* whether the document is short enough to be read on-screen or should be printed out;
* the per-page rate for printing out PDFs;

* whether to return the paper proofs or mark the PDFs using the standard marks embedded with PaperlessProofs.

When proofreaders will be reading against the original hard copy and the project has multiple elements – for example, artwork, separate copy for captions and tables – you can update the editorial handover form, deleting items that are not being included, and dating any changes. However, when there are few elements, or when proofreaders are reading 'blind', you do not need to send the handover form, because you are not sending the material shown on it. Then in your letter or e-mail you can simply list the proofs and items such as the AIS and style sheets, which provide the relevant background.

The letter should state whether the proofreading is against copy or blind. Competent proofreaders know what is expected of them in each case, but reminding them of key tasks that do not occur on every job or that you want done in a particular way is a good idea.

Exercise 5.2: Briefing a proofreader

Claire did all that was asked in copy-editing *Here's to Your Health!* and returned the job on time. You keyed in the photos on the new hard copy, added the caption file to the e-files and hard copy, and sent the materials to design and production on schedule. The artwork has been scanned into the proofs but spaces have been left for a few late photos. The photos will not be numbered in the book, so you have circled their keying-in numbers on the caption copy.

Although you have chosen Tom to proofread against copy and to collate, you have never worked with him before. You will be sending paper proofs on schedule. Using information about the project in this and earlier chapters, write a brief for Tom.

Even though Claire has input the editorial changes, asking Tom to mark editorial corrections in blue and typesetting errors in red is useful: it provides feedback on Claire's editorial and keyboarding skills, and reveals any instances where the typesetter has applied the wrong style. If Tom were also going to be collating the authors' changes, you could ask him to mark these in black, which would enable excessive corrections to be charged to the authors and would provide a clear record if the source of any changes were to be questioned later. Alternatively, you could tell Tom the maximum number of editorial and author corrections allowed in the budget and ask him to keep within that limit or to indicate why, and how many, extra changes are needed.

Because there are blank spaces where the photos will be, Tom needs to transfer the numbers from the hard copy. Reminding him to check the numbers against those on the caption copy should ensure that there are no mistakes if the designer has had to place the photos out of numerical sequence.

The scheduling dates have to include when Tom can expect the authors' proofs, so that he can plan his time for reading and for collating. When you send authors' proofs to be collated, remember to give the editor or proofreader guidance on the level of change that is acceptable to keep the authors happy and yet remain in budget. Tom is not given dates for the revised proofs, because you will be checking those yourself. It does not take long and it is a key stage – passing proofs for press – so be sure to put it 'on your schedule.

For indexers

When you first discuss a job with an indexer, you will cover the subject and intended audience and the length of the work being indexed, the type of index or indexes, as well as the schedule and the fee. When proofs are being sent as PDFs, you should also agree the rate per page for printing them out if that is how the indexer works. Use an AIS to confirm some of this information and a letter for the rest. You could include all the other detail indexers need in the same letter or send them another index in the same style, but to save your time and theirs, and to avoid oversights, use a style sheet or, if the projects on which you work require a variety of styles, a checklist for general points (see Fig. 5.4). Either of these should include guidance on:

* capitalization
* alphabetization
* punctuation
* layout style
* nature of locators
* numeral style
* style for reference to illustrations
* delivery format

INDEXING CHECKLIST

Title: _____ Author: _____

Alphabetize
❑ letter by letter
❑ word by word

Capitalize
❑ all entries
❑ proper nouns only

Levels
❑ main entries only
❑ subentries
❑ sub-subentries

Layout
❑ broken off
❑ run on
❑ line space between sections of alphabet
❑ capital letter between sections of alphabet

Indent
❑ subentries ____ spaces
❑ turnovers ____ spaces

Locators
❑ page numbers
❑ paragraph numbers
❑ section numbers
❑ clause numbers

Punctuation
❑ space only after entries
❑ colon after main entries
❑ comma after main entries
❑ comma between subentries and locators

Numeral style
❑ full
❑ elided except for numbers ending in 0: 22–3 but 30–31
❑ all elided: 30–1

Reference to illustrations
❑ italic
❑ bold
❑ hyperlink
❑ other: _____

Special instructions
❑ chronological subentries for events
❑ exclude non-substantive references
❑ other: _____

Extent
___ characters per line
___ lines

Delivery
❑ hard copy
❑ by e-mail to [address]
❑ software: _____

Figure 5.4 A checklist for briefing indexers

The letter or form must also state how long the index should be. A good index can be ruined by someone other than the indexer trying to cut or expand it afterwards. Consult the designer or typesetter to work out the length of the index. The specifications state the number of words and the number of pages. Designers can work out how many pages will be occupied by prelims, text and illustrations, and end matter, and therefore how many pages are available for the index. Consider the size of the index relative to the length and complexity of the work and the level of readership. Do

Index

Figure 5.5 Sample index page

you have enough space for the index in broken-off layout? It's easier to use but takes up more space than run-on style. Do you have an existing index design that you can use to plan the length? If not, ask the designer to show you some alternatives in column width and typesize. Then tell the indexer how many characters to a line and how many lines are available.

Although you could put all the information, including the schedule and the fee, on the form, keeping some details for the letter provides an opportunity for a more personal communication.

Exercise 5.3 Briefing an indexer

> Zara will index *Here's to Your Health!*. There are eight pages available for the index. Use the example in figure 5.5 (from another index in the style and specification you want) as a basis for completing the checklist. Use the schedule from Exercise 5.1 and the information here and in previous chapters to write a brief for Zara.

The style of the existing index is clear. The characters per line are determined by counting the longest line, as in any unjustified setting. Determining the number of lines is simple arithmetic. A full column has 56 lines – you must include the heading, because on other pages the columns will start at this point, the top of the text area. There are 3 columns on a page ($56 \times 3 = 168$), and 8 pages ($168 \times 8 = 1344$), but the columns on the page with the heading have only 54 lines ($1344 - 6 = 1338$).

The answer sheet asks for hard copy and e-files, but you could have opted for printing your own hard copy to edit and mark up. In either case you needed to state the program. Many indexers use special software programs but export the files as Word or RTF (rich text format), the latter often presenting fewer problems moving across platforms. When you're not sure what is required, check with production.

The schedule is easy to determine: the indexer needs page proofs to work on and you need the index in time for it to be edited and sent for setting with the corrected pages. Although choosing the indexer, negotiating the fee and setting the schedule are always your responsibility, you can delegate the briefing and editing to the copy-editor.

You should be aware that, like all authors (that is, creators of original work), indexers have copyright in their work and, unless they agree to sell it, this should be stated in the same place as other copyright ownership in the work. Even when copyright owners sell their copyright, they have the right (one of the 'moral rights' in copyright acts throughout the European Union) to be identified as the creator of that work. In countries where this is not enshrined in law, it is still the reasonable thing to do. Although you don't need to mention it in the letter, remember to put an AIS in the package.

For illustrators

Illustrators can use the information about the target audience on the AIS to help decide on the degree of detail and sophistication for the images generally. If the publication market is international, illustrators need to be told if there are any restrictions on what may be depicted or any requirements for people or objects to be represented in a particular way.

Briefs should confirm the general style for artwork, which has usually been decided at the beginning of projects, although you will most probably have to determine, in consultation with the design or production manager, the detail concerning annotations and presentation. These requirements can be described in a memo or on a checklist (Fig. 5.6) and, if the work is to follow a series style, by giving illustrators copies of existing publications.

Authors might describe the artwork they want, provide their own sketches or photocopy illustrations from another source. Whoever is briefing the illustrator, you or a copy-editor, has to evaluate an author's materials in order to prepare the briefs for individual figures. Pare down descriptions to a list of essential visual elements, then read it back to yourself to see if it conveys the image the author intends. Examine references to ensure that the editorial content for each figure is complete – everything that must be shown is there – clear and consistent with the text. When illustrators will be making some creative contribution, make sure that the briefs state clearly anything that must not be included in the images. Essential omissions are usually determined by the sales markets.

Not all illustrations need references; it may depend not only on the specific content of the image but also on the experience or

---

PROJECT STYLE

Title:_____ Author:_____

Illustrations
___ line
___ tone

___ black only
___ other monochrome colour _____
___ 2nd colour _____
___ full colour _____

❏ squared with rules
❏ squared without rules
❏ vignetted
❏ silhouetted _____
❏ bleeding
❏ not bleeding

___ representational
___ abstract
___ cartoon
___ realia
___ diagram

Working size
❏ ss
❏ ×0.5
❏ ×1.5
❏ ×2
❏ other _____

Annotations
❏ typed, marked-up list(s) attached
❏ plain lines to subjects
❏ arrows to subjects
❏ black only
❏ 2nd colour _____
❏ reverse out
❏ in separate file/on overlay

Electronic delivery
software _____
palette requirements _____

❏ e-mail to _____
❏ CD

Hard copy presentation
materials

_____

Schedule
Visuals by _____
Final a/w by _____

Figure 5.6 A checklist for artwork. Write the appropriate number in the spaces before the category, tick boxes where the category applies to all illustrations, and provide relevant information in spaces after the item.

specialization of the illustrator. Use your common sense and when in doubt, ask the illustrator or design manager. When illustrations from other copyright sources are being used as references, illustrators must be reminded not to copy, or even adapt, them unless you are getting permission to do so, but to use the information to create a new image. In all cases, annotation should be typed and marked up for illustrators, who are not expected to do this themselves.

If your artwork briefs differ significantly from the authors', send copies to them, drawing attention to the changes you have suggested, just as you would a copy-edited text. Get their approval or agree changes before sending the briefs to the illustrator.

Briefs for individual illustrations should state the reproduction size, either the proportion of the defined page or precise dimensions. The working size might be proportionately larger. Figure 5.6 shows the most common working sizes: ss, same size as reproduction; × 0.5, half size of reproduction; × 1.5, often called 'half up'; and × 2, or twice up.

Briefs for the entire job should, of course, include schedule dates for receipt and return of artists' visuals, and for final artwork; and the fee for the job. When illustrators retain copyright, the brief must state what the fee covers. For example, is the licence for one use only or can the illustrations be used in revised editions and other formats? Is the artwork to be returned to the artist at a specific time after use or retained by the client? When the client is buying the illustrator's copyright, the agreement must be in writing. Otherwise the illustrator's copyright should be shown on the copyright page. Remember that even when illustrators sell their copyright, they – like other copyright owners in the European Union – have the right to be identified as the creator of that work (see page 86). It is worth repeating that in countries where the observance of this moral right is not enshrined in law, it is still the reasonable thing to do.

Exercise 5.4: Creating artwork briefs

An illustrator has been chosen for *Here's to Your Health!* and been given the AIS. Brief the illustrator to produce artwork for:
1 the figure in Exercise 3.2, and
2 the figure for which the author has provided the notes and rough opposite.

Complete the artwork checklist in Figure 5.6 as if these were the only illustrations in the book. Refer to Exercise 5.1 for relevant dates. The specification does not allow for bleeds. Ignore the technical information about working size, delivery and presentation, which the designer will fill in. The design manager will also negotiate the fees.

Outdoor fitness trail — a marked run with exercises about every 100 metres, with instruction boards at each.

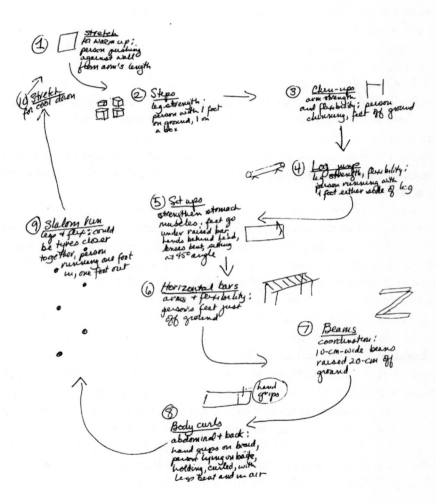

① Stretch
for warm up:
person pushing
against wall
from arm's length

⑩ Stretch
for cool down

② Steps
leg strength:
person with 1 foot
on ground, 1 on
a box

③ Chin-ups
arm strength
and flexibility: person
chinning, feet off ground

④ Log jump
leg strength, flexibility:
person running with
1 foot either side of log

⑤ Sit ups
strengthen stomach
muscles: feet go
under raised bar,
hands behind head,
knees bent, sitting
at 45° angle

⑨ Slalom run
legs + flips: could
be tyres closer
together, person
running one foot
in, one foot out

⑥ Horizontal bars
arms + flexibility:
person's feet just
off ground

⑦ Beams
coordination:
10-cm-wide beams
raised 20-cm off
ground

hand grips

⑧ Body curls
abdominal + back:
hand grips on board,
person lying on back,
holding, curled, with
legs bent and in air

The answer sheet has chosen a squared without rules style, but you are free to choose with rules or vignetted. However, you had to tick the 'not bleeding' box because that is the brief you were given.

Because the book will be produced in more than one language, the annotation must not be reversed out through all four colours. Therefore it must be presented on a separate layer or in a separate file from the illustration. It will, in fact, be on the text black plate, separate from the black plate for the illustrations; in this way each language edition can use the same illustrations, which is the basis of co-edition publishing.

The illustrator needs to know how much space each illustration will occupy. If you had the page plan, you could provide exact dimensions. In this case the brief said the designer will give the page plan to the illustrator, so you can give the sizes as a proportion of the page. The amount of detail in each illustration should indicate the amount of space it will need. The pie chart might fit into one-sixth of a page.

Your brief for the diagram might be more creative than the one in the answer, but the point is to eliminate the author's bullet list by putting the information in the illustration. Remove the squared background, a feature of some word-processing programs, by drawing a line through the corners and noting it in the brief. If the style were squared with rules, the illustrator would enclose the pie chart and annotation within a much larger ruled area than that shown here.

The brief for the fitness trail needs to itemize essential additions – human figure, instruction boards – and clarify the background, order and scale. Highlighting those of the author's notes that will help the illustrator saves time because the latter can ignore the other writing.

The schedule dates were worked out in Exercise 5.1. You, not the copy-editor, are checking the visuals, so you just needed to pick the right date. Do not ask for work before a weekend or public holiday, since you won't be doing anything with it then and the person producing it might need the time to complete it.

For photographers

Like artwork, commissioned photographs are unique images. The similarity in the briefs is that they must describe the essential content of the image – which needs to be complete, clear and consistent with the text – and any essential omissions. The difference is that there are no 'visuals' to approve, no opportunity to make changes. Even if you go to the shoot, trying to alter detail then can cause confusion, frustration and delay, and increase costs.

Try to visualize each photograph that is needed, then describe the format (portrait or landscape), if essential, and the detail. Stipulate whether all the photos are to be in colour or in black and white, or, if mixed, identify the minority group. Send the briefs to the author and set your copies aside for a day or two – make sure you schedule time to do this – then discuss with the author the images the briefs suggest. If you have delegated creating the briefs to the copy-editor, check them to make sure you can visualize the photographs.

Hand over the briefs far enough in advance of the shoot for stylists to obtain necessary props, accessories and costumes; for photographers to locate appropriate settings; and for you to check with them that the briefs are clear, complete and understood.

As well as the schedule, briefs must state, as for artwork, what usage the fee covers, who owns the copyright and who retains the photographs after use. Photographers, like all creators of literary and visual material, have a legal right to be identified with their work even if they sell their copyright.

Exercise 5.5: Preparing briefs for photographs

Two hundred of the photographs for *Here's to Your Health!* are to be commissioned. Below are the captions for photographs that will accompany three exercises and some comments from Alex Ciser. It has been agreed that the models will be fitness trainers, to ensure that the positions are correct, and that the setting should look like a sitting room rather than a gym. Prepare briefs for the photographs.

You do not have the budget information, but work out the schedule on the form used in Exercise 5.1.

Ex. 7

1   Stand leg length away from a thigh-high stable support, such as a desk or chest of drawers. Turn your right leg out slightly. Raise your left leg to the front and brace your heel on the support. Lean forward to grasp your heel with both hands.

2   Lean over and try to touch your forehead to your knee. Flex your foot
    for a count of five, point for a count of five, then flex for a count of
    five. Lower your left leg.
Repeat with the right leg.

> The model's head should not come really close to the knee – that
> discourages beginners. Complete body line is important; head is always
> facing same way as body unless caption says otherwise. Safety is
> important, so support shouldn't be anything that might tip when weight
> is placed on it. Alex

Ex. 8

1   Stand with your feet just over shoulder-width apart, knees bent and
    toes turned diagonally out. Place your hands behind your head with
    your elbows back.
2   Bend your knees so that your thighs are as close to horizontal as
    possible, keeping your heels on the ground and buttocks tightened.
    Hold for a count of five, making sure your buttocks don't drop below
    knee level. Relax, then rise to your toes for a count of five, keeping
    buttocks and thighs tightened.
3   Lower your heels to the ground. Bend sideways from the waist towards
    your right knee. Hold for a count of five. Straighten, then bend to the
    left and hold for a count of five.

Ex. 9

1   Standing straight or sitting on your bare feet, raise your left arm
    straight up and bend your elbow so that your palm touches your left
    shoulder blade. Press your right hand with palm forward against your
    left elbow and push your elbow back for a count of 10.
2   Extend your left arm straight above your head with your palm forward,
    keeping your right arm where it was. Stretch up for a count of 10, then
    return to the starting position.
Repeat with your right arm.

Of course you remembered to check the AIS (Exercise 3.3), which
says that all the photographs are in colour.

The author has noted that 'body line is important', so you should
put the note about the direction of the head into the general brief.
Seeing the pictures in your head, you might have realized that the
models' outfits, in fit and in colour, must enhance rather than obscure

the body line. Bare feet make pointing and flexing the feet easier to see too.

Alex is also concerned about safety. The shoot will be in a studio, with props specially arranged. Think about items that could be safety hazards and exclude them.

Using the captions as briefs saves time and provides context for the fitness trainers being used as models. Highlighting the parts that show the stance focuses the photographer's attention on the image. The view instructions are vital. Without them, the photos of Exercise 7 could show the model from the left, with the position of the right leg obscured; and the photos of Exercise 9 could show the model from the front, missing the detail of the hand touching the shoulder blade. Using a note in the general brief to cover the view in the majority of photos avoids unnecessary repetition and keeps details in individual briefs to a minimum.

It will not take very long to prepare the briefs in this case, because the author's captions serve as the basis, but the schedule allows for the fact that other work is being done at the same time. Similarly, the period for the shoot itself is the time within which the work must be done. It may be started later and finished sooner – that is the photographer's decision; it simply must not be finished late.

For picture researchers

Picture researchers always need to know the
* author(s) name(s)
* title of the work
* specifications
* estimated selling price
* estimated print run
* publication markets

Once again, the AIS provides all this basic information and more, which helps to put the job in context and might provide clues as to the desired quality or rarity of images, their probable sources and costs, and the adequacy of the schedule. Later, picture researchers will also need to know the reproduction size and use of each image – for example, for the cover, blad or inside the book – because they negotiate permissions and reproduction rights for the photos they locate, and this is the information on which the sources will base their fees.

PICTURE RESEARCH BRIEFING FORM

Title: _____   Author: _____

Picture researchers are expected to:

1 Pre-select photos for good reproduction quality.
2 Check invoices agree with fees and terms negotiated.
3 Provide complete and accurate picture credits for each image.
4 Package CDs or other materials to ensure they will not be damaged in transit.
5 Hand over complete and accurate documentation to the client at the end of the project.
6 Immediately inform the project manager of any problems that might affect the choice of illustrations, the schedule or the budget.
7 Provide receipts and records of expenses.

and for non-digital photos:

8 Check incoming materials and return damaged items to sources immediately.
9 Check delivery notes on receipt for accuracy and inform sources of errors immediately.
10 Keep a log to ensure location of materials is known at all times.
11 Take all necessary steps to ensure that holding fees are not incurred.
12 Return transparencies to sources after use, accompanied by an accurate delivery note.
13 Pay loss or damage fees for materials in their possession.

On this project you are requested to:

❑ research _____ subjects in colour, _____ in black-and-white

❑ acquire the specific photographs listed by _____

❑ acquire a sufficient number of photographs of the subjects listed for initial selection

   by _____ and final selection by _____

❑ acquire photos that have not been published often

❑ acquire any relevant information for captions from sources

❑ negotiate copyright permissions and reproduction fees _____ markets and within the budget of

   _____

❑ provide a complete and accurate list of picture credits for publication

❑ mark up a file copy of the book

❑ send materials by agreed courier service

❑ send materials by special delivery/registered post with adequate insurance

❑ liaise with _____

The client will:

1 Provide a comprehensive list of photographs required.
2 Provide a copy of the text when necessary.
3 Assume responsibility for the condition of materials while in the possession of its staff or subcontractors, and pay loss or damage fees incurred by any of these parties.
4 Comply with the terms and conditions agreed with the sources and pay their invoices on publication.

Figure 5.7 A picture research briefing form

Briefs should provide not only essential information but also, when possible, an opportunity for picture researchers to make a creative contribution. It is essential for a picture list to state the subject of each photo and, like illustrators' and photographers' briefs, the elements that must be included in and excluded from it to convey the author's message. That's simple when the pictures wanted are unique and from specified sources. For example, for a particular work of art in a museum the list needs to state:

* the name of the artist
* the title of the work
* its location, if known

When there is, or might be, more than one work of the same title by the same artist, you would need to add the date and medium, such as watercolour or oil painting, bronze or marble sculpture.

Perhaps any type of work by a particular artist is wanted. Then the most useful information would be the

* name of the artist
* media in which she or he worked
* location(s) of major collections of her or his work

The range of potential information increases when the subjects are more general. Sometimes authors specify photographs they've seen in other publications. Always check whether it is those photos or the subject matter that is really wanted. Then look at the detail requested, if any. Let's say the subjects are particular places. Look for any information in the text or from the author that indicates whether it is necessary or desirable that the photos show these places:

* from particular angles
* at day or night
* in a specific season or year
* with or without people, traffic or specific landmarks

Specify only important elements on the list, then provide researchers with a copy of the text and any existing visual materials (other publications in the series or sample spreads, for example), and allow them to exercise their creative faculties to bring you a selection of visually exciting images of the subject.

When only certain photos are to be in colour, indicate which they are. Similarly, if you know that images are to be used very large or very small, let researchers know, so that they can choose originals that have the appropriate qualities for that reproduction.

Be prepared to discuss lists after picture researchers have had time to assess them. Researchers might want to clarify points, get more detail or explain to you limitations, such as the availability of colour for certain subjects before a specific date and the slow response or pre-payment requirements of some sources.

As well as confirming the schedule and the budget for the use of photos, briefs must make clear mutual responsibilities for administrative work, such as handling and returning non-digital photos when required, approving and paying invoices, and preparing acknowledgements. This can also be done easily with a standard form, such as the one in Figure 5.7. The covering letter can then confirm the researcher's fee and any special instructions, such as your availability or details about picture-selection meetings.

Exercise 5.6 Briefing a picture researcher

In Unit 4 we chose Michael to research the pictures for *Here's to Your Health!* The budget for the photos is 1500 and Michael has agreed to a fee of 2800 to cover research, selection meetings, returns and all the usual administrative detail.

Work out, or check what you put on, the schedule used in Exercise 5.5. Use Figure 5.7 as part of the brief and put other information in a letter. The subjects below come from the sample chapter in Exercise 3.2. Add any information necessary or helpful.

1 Super-thin celebrities
2 People different shapes and sizes
3 Apple- and pear-shaped people
4 People playing sports
5 People eating healthy meals

Michael needs a copy of the text for context because the subjects are so generally described and because you want him to make a creative contribution. The letter draws Michael's attention to the ramifications of the sales markets given on the form as well as confirming his fee and encouraging him to get in touch if he has any queries or wants to discuss any issues.

The form covers the other general points. The AIS says there are 300 photos, all in full colour, and Exercise 5.5 said 200 of them would be commissioned, leaving 100 subjects to be sourced. The AIS also states which rights have been sold. You might have put 'world English language, French, Italian' for markets, but it is more sensible to cover the possibility that other rights will be sold rather than have to clear them for individual countries later.

Your first selection date might not be exactly the same as the one on the answer, but it's OK as long as you've left some time for a few gaps to be filled. Remember, there could be more time to get in the actual photos if copies or photocopies can be used for selection.

The individual picture briefs follow the principles of noting essential inclusions and essential omissions. The first picture requires international celebrities because of the sales markets, and established models would be best because they can be said to have remained super-thin and celebrities for a known period, whereas the celebrity of this year's models might not stand the test of time, and the weight of other types of celebrities might fluctuate.

The preferred shot is given for the second and third picture; you had to think that there are two possibilities, but you might have chosen the other one in each case. Clarification of 'different shapes and sizes' for the second picture is to ensure that the photo is consistent with the authors' message about healthy norms.

The additions to the brief for picture 4 are to ensure a balanced view for any sales market, and the information about the food and background in the fifth subject is, again, to make sure the search is for photos that will be consistent with the text.

6 Supervising

Supervising the work other people are doing should enable you to spot and resolve problems at an early stage and thus ensure that the project reaches fruition on schedule, within budget and to the specified quality. Although you might choose to do some editorial tasks yourself (see Chapter 4), when you delegate work to other people, your job is to check what they have done, not to do it yourself.

Communicating

Communication is the underlying principle of publishing and of all the work that you do. You have, of course, established lines of communication with all the team members by the time you have completed the briefings, and you have become aware that communication means listening to what others have to say as well as imparting information to them. Now, and throughout the life of the project, you must strengthen and maintain those lines of communication.

Some people are not good communicators: they might not be able to focus on the relevant information and express their thoughts clearly, accurately or concisely; or they might not take the initiative to relate information, but always wait to be asked. To manage the project smoothly, you must be a good communicator and take responsibility for communication: tell your colleagues what they need to know in order to do their jobs well, and find ways to ensure that they tell you everything you need to know when you need to know it. You can optimize your time by briefing some people to report to you at specified intervals or stages in the project: the general invitation to 'contact me if there is anything you wish to discuss' is not always a strong enough motivator. If people fail to report at the specified times, contact them, and note this trait. You may want to use these individuals again because of their other skills, and it will be to your advantage to be aware of, and prepared for, their inability to follow this part of the brief.

Checking schedules

Preceding chapters have made clear how important it is to stay in touch with authors throughout the project to monitor schedules and provide support. You must always take the initiative in maintaining these relationships. To establish a framework for communication, annotate your scheduling form with dates to contact authors:

* prior to submission to check delivery will be on time;
* after delivery to acknowledge it and review the copy-editing procedures, emphasizing the importance of making all changes during this stage because they will not be allowed at proof;
* prior to sending out proofs to warn of their arrival and to remind authors of the return date and that they should mark corrections to mistakes only;
* to arrange predetermined meetings, for example, to select or check illustrations.

Obviously, you might need to contact authors at other times too, but these dates are all dictated by publishing processes.

When you, the design manager and production manager work in-house, regular scheduling meetings, particularly when you are managing several projects, are an efficient use of time. Leading a meeting, you can impart essential information, ask very specific questions to get precisely the information you know you want and, if necessary, prompt your colleagues to respond with any other relevant points. Having these meetings on the same day of the week and at the same time helps all of you to remember, plan for and be able to attend them. If you or these two key colleagues are freelance, individual phone calls or conference calls can replace such meetings.

Similarly, you can instruct the other team members to contact you at a specific time to report on their progress. This can be done by e-mail if the information is simple and unequivocal – for example, 'text to design on schedule'; otherwise, speaking to people has the advantage of enabling you to check immediately that what you or they have said is accurately interpreted and clearly understood, and to discuss any points that might need clarification or further action. As for meetings, arranging a set day and time – even as general as 'morning' or 'afternoon' – for these communications establishes a framework for action, and signals you to contact others when you don't hear from them. Following telephone calls, confirm the conclusions concisely by e-mail, and date and file your copy.

Staying focused on scheduling will help you get the information you need and keep meetings, phone calls and e-mails short. If issues that do not relate to the schedule arise, defer them to the end of the meeting or call, then deal with them one at a time to maximize everyone's concentration and minimize the expenditure of time.

Checking schedules with design and production should be done weekly or fortnightly. Because these colleagues are responsible for the manufacturing stages, they need to be kept up to date with the progress of the project even before it is in their hands. Once the materials are in production, of course, you want to check that the schedule is being maintained.

How often you need to check progress with other team members will be relative to the length of their involvement in the project and your knowledge of their reliability. For example, if the editing were to be allocated five months, you might want monthly reports from a copy-editor with whom you've never worked, but reports every six or even eight weeks from one you know always delivers punctually. Proofreaders and indexers usually have short schedules, so you might find it useful to contact them only a few days before delivery is due to check that it will be on time. When you get to know them well and are sure of their reliability – especially, when you can depend on them to contact you if a problem arises or a delay threatens – you may find it is not necessary to check their progress at all.

Even if you delegate briefing and selecting illustrations to the copy-editor, you might want to attend picture-selection meetings. This enables you to check progress as well as the quality of the images being selected. You will usually schedule two such meetings with picture researchers – a preliminary and a final one. It is a good idea to check a few days in advance with researchers you don't know that there will be enough images to make the meeting useful. Too few images is an indication that the schedule might be in danger. Discussing the reasons for this is important but having a meeting could waste time better spent addressing the problem.

Delays, potential and actual

'Slippage' and 'delay' are two of the ugliest words in publishing, along with their close associates 'extra costs' and 'lost profits'. Chapter 1 made clear that creating a realistic schedule is essential. Of course that's no guarantee that everything will happen as planned. No one plans to get ill or have equipment break down, but these and many other unexpected problems can occur. Knowing at the earliest moment what the problem is and being able to assess what its impact on the schedule might be are the keys to preventing or minimizing delays. That is why you check schedules regularly and brief everyone to let you know as soon as a potential delay is spotted.

Make dealing with potential delays the top priority: resolve them quickly rather than adding to them. When you are notified of a potential or imminent delay, find out:

* the cause;
* the length;
* what action, if any, the informant suggests.

Then assess the effect of the projected delay on the critical path and on the subsidiary paths. Ask yourself the following questions to determine the best cousrse of action.

1 Can contingency time in this stage absorb some or all of the delay?
2 Can another stage in the procedure absorb some or all of the delay?
3 Will using extra or replacement personnel or equipment prevent or minimize the delay?
4 Will action suggested by another team member prevent or minimize the delay?
5 Is the cost of the solution within your budget?
6 Is exceeding the budget preferable to the consequences of the delay?

For example, if someone on the editorial team is ill or a computer has broken down and the resulting delay will be short – a few days – the solution might be points 1 and 2. Check with other team members to see whether they will be able and are willing to do their work in a shorter period of time than originally agreed, and, if so, whether that would mean working overtime and add to costs.

If the causes are the same but the resulting delay will be weeks, point 3 might be more appropriate: can you split a job between two people or lend a laptop? If that's not the answer, consult the other members of the team who will be affected by the delay as soon as possible – point 4 – even if you think you have the best solution worked out. They might offer you a better one – perhaps there are different processes or technologies that will save time – or confirm that yours is the best one. In either case, of course, they need to be kept informed.

Points 5 and 6 remind you that time and money are inextricably linked. You might have to balance the prospect of running over budget with that of losing sales and market share.

If you can't prevent a delay, try to minimize it. When a delay will affect the publication date, you must inform marketing, publicity and sales as soon as possible. You might not be able to prevent lost sales, but you might save the time, effort and money that would otherwise have been wasted on promoting a title that will not be available.

Exercise 6.1: Dealing with delays

Here are three situations for you to deal with. Make a list of the actions you might take in each case.

A On what you expect to be your last phone call to the author before delivery, the author says not all the materials will be ready on time. She thinks she can finish the text in another two weeks. The commissioning editor, whom you would normally consult before making a decision, is on holiday. What do you do?

B The author has not returned his proofs on the due date. The proofs need to be collated and sent for correction in a few days. What do you do?

C The proofreader phones you halfway through the time allocated for the job – a 448-page book. He had done about 10 per cent of the work before he became ill. He had hoped he would recover in time to complete it but now realizes he won't. What do you do?

Your answers might be more elaborate than those on the answer sheet but should include the basic actions listed there. For A, you need to gather the information (points 1 and 2) that will help you to assess the situation (4 and 5). Point 3 is multifold. Making the author aware of the problems that might ensue, including damage to sales of her book, might provoke her into thinking how she can help mini-mize the delay. Even if that is not possible, because of the nature of the cause, it lets her know the problems you have to resolve and that you need time to do it. If work can begin on the incomplete mater-ials (4), you can take the pressure off the author and avoid delay. Nonetheless, address point 5. If the cause of the delay has been the author's miscalculation of how much she could achieve in a given period, she might need more than the time she is estimating now. However, if the cause is a short-term problem – a cold or a computer problem – you might be able to persuade her to make up for lost time more quickly. Always consult these colleagues: tell them the nature of the problem and your suggested solutions. They might be able to offer you a little time from their schedules, or at least be pre-pared for the delay. Whatever decisions you make, you must, of course, inform the author (7).

The first action in B is obviously to contact him; this would be the quickest way to find out what you need to know. Leaving messages in two ways doubles your chances of getting a timely response. Note that you are asking for information: do not assume that the author has neglected his responsibility. Check the contract (2) so that you are sure and can, if necessary, remind the author that point 3a is agreed. If the author has been told from the beginning that changes to proofs are for corrections of errors only and all queries have been resolved at copy-editing, there are likely to be few, if any, substantive changes, so the author is likely to remember them. Thus, in 3b as in 3a, you can return the proofs on time.

Take action 1 in C not only because it is appropriate but also to reinforce the importance of reporting delays. Responsible people feel badly about failing to fulfil their obligations and worry what this might mean in terms of future work. Being grateful that you still have time to solve the problem rather than being irritated that it has arisen strengthens your relationship with the proofreader. Some jobs – for example, those where chapters or sections are not interdependent – can be split between proofreaders, but if the copy-editor rather than you is collating the proofs, brief him or her to be extra careful about consistency. The rest is common sense.

During your career you may have to deal with many kinds of potential delays. Knowing that you have created a realistic schedule, have a sound understanding of the processes of producing a publication and are a good communicator will help you to do so calmly. And remember: **always discuss potential delays as soon as possible with all the colleagues who might be affected by them.**

Checking quality

You are responsible for ensuring that the project you produce on time is of the quality required. Your selection of the people to do the work and your briefs are two key elements in achieving this goal. The third is monitoring the work. You should allocate time in the schedule to attend handover and illustrations meetings, and to check the work done by each team member before you send it on to the next stage. How much time you allow for the latter depends on:

* the amount of time you have available;
* the complexity and quality of the project;
* the qualities and experience of the team members;
* your experience generally and of the work of the team members specifically – be careful not to confuse knowing people with knowing their work.

To make the best use of the time you have available, plan your work.

Copy-editing

Effective project management depends on the ability to delegate. Of course you must know how to copy-edit in order to check the work being done. Remember, however, that you have entrusted this task to someone else and that no two individuals would make all the same decisions. You might have done the job differently, you might prefer different stylistic choices, but as long as what the copy-editor has done has made the author's message clear to the reader and provides the quality of finished product required, don't tamper with it. If there are errors, they need to be corrected – by you or the copy-editor, depending on their nature and the time available – but other changes to satisfy your preferences are counter-productive: you risk introducing errors and inconsistencies that have to be corrected later, perhaps endangering your budget, overriding agreements with the author, undermining the copy-editor's authority and diminishing the quality of his or her work, and thus alienating two of your team members; and wasting your time. Don't do it.

Instead, decide how often you will need to check the work. (Please note the future tense: planning facilitates doing.) On a project where the copy-editing will take months and you are not familiar with the copy-editor's work, you should plan to check the work when a relatively small proportion of it has been completed. If there are elements that have not been encountered or dealt with at that stage, such as tables or references, plan another interim check; otherwise, if satisfied with the quality, check the whole job at the end. Your safeguard is that you have briefed the copy-editor to raise any problems with you at any time, and you can always inquire about the project generally when you are checking schedules. You might want to follow the same procedure even when you have confidence in a copy-editor's work if the project is especially complex, must be of high quality, or is especially important to the publisher.

When several copy-editors are working simultaneously on the same project, which happens, for example, on single and multi-volume encyclopedias, it is important to check the work reasonably early and at intervals to make sure that the outcome will be consistent in detail and style.

Next, determine what you will be looking for. Start by framing questions based on the brief you gave, as in Figure 6.1. Notice that all the questions are aimed at checking that the work required has been done and is clear and appropriate. Do not read the entire edited material but look at samples. Check a few random paragraphs that have been rewritten or added to answer the questions raised. Look at the hard copy or tracked e-file to assess the extent of cuts, and read a few sections at random to check the standard of the remaining text. Look at all the briefs to answer the questions shown in the figure. Check a few in detail to be sure they are consistent with the text.

Now check selected bits of text for the standard of general copy-editing: clarity in presentation as well as content, concision, accuracy, and consistency. Do it efficiently by focusing on discrete elements. Do it first, say, with headings. Review the tables next. Then survey first paragraphs and different types of text, such as displayed material, notes, and cross-references. Check the punctuation and application of house style in random paragraphs. Finally, read a chunk of text for its style: clear, flowing, and without unnecessary repetition.

In all these cases read a little more, or in more detail, only if you are not satisfied, so that you can assess what is wrong. Even so, you

COPY-EDITING ASSESSMENT

Brief:	Check whether:
Rewrite specified matter	■ it has been done ■ it improves the clarity of the text ■ it retains the author's voice ■ it is at the right level
Cut text by X per cent	■ it has been done ■ all essential information has been retained ■ the remaining text is smooth, cohesive and coherent
Expand text by X per cent	■ it has been done ■ the additional information is appropriate and substantive ■ the additional information is in the author's voice and blends into the text seamlessly
Prepare permissions list	■ it has been done ■ the information is complete ■ the list is presented clearly
Prepare artwork briefs	■ it has been done ■ each brief is given a figure number ■ each brief is clear and concise ■ each brief includes any required reference material ■ each brief shows position of any annotation ■ all annotation is neatly typed and marked up

Figure 6.1 Creating a checklist based on the brief

will not have to read the entire text. If you spot minor errors – a misspelling or missing punctuation mark – during a preliminary check, correct them and return the work to the copy-editor with a note so that he or she will review what has been done and be more careful in completing the job. If there are more serious errors at this stage, highlight them, contact the editor to discuss what must be done to improve the work, and then return the material to the editor to revise. Check this person's work again before the job is due to be completed. When errors are found only when you are checking the completed job, there probably will not be sufficient time to allow the copy-editor to make the corrections. Do this yourself carefully, disciplining yourself only to correct, not make unnecessary changes, and make a note for use in feedback.

Exercise 6.2: Checking the copy-editing

For an introductory book on botany aimed at the 14–16 age range, the copy-editor was briefed to do a medium edit, and told that the author was very weak on punctuation. The brief also noted that space was tight and the text should not be expanded. The copy-editor has returned this tracked excerpt from the chapter titled 'In the beginning' after agreeing all substantive changes with the author. The underlining indicates new or revised text. In the briefed system of electronic mark-up the usual coding is preceded by @ and followed by a colon closed up to the next character.

This is a very small sample of work and so it is easy to read it through. Instead, check specific aspects of the work: list what you have looked at and your assessment of it.

The main elements of the house style are:
* -ize spellings
* initial cap for Earth as planet name
* numbers 10 and above as numerals
* a comma between the hundreds and thousands in numbers of four or more digits
* single quotes

@A:~~The~~ Algae~~:~~ ~~seaweeds~~

Algae, together with bacteria and fungi, represent the earliest forms of life on Earth. ~~Fossillised~~ Fossilized algae ~~dating three thousand~~3000 million years ~~ago~~old are found in some rocks and are the oldest fossils known. Most algae are aquatic and found in the sea either as plankton, the drifting mass of minute plant and animal life that is so important as a food for many species of fish, or seaweeds.

@B:Seaweeds

There are various ways of classifying seaweeds. One ~~which is~~useful classification, which is also based on technical characteristics, is into colour groups. So at a glance we can tell whether we are looking at the red algae, the brown algae or the green algae. The green species grow where there is most sunlight, just under the surface of the sea. At lower depths, where only the green and blue light rays of the sun penetrate, the brown and red algae thrive because they use these light rays to make their food.

Seaweeds are found throughout the world's oceans~~. and because~~Because
they are ~~the~~most plentiful near the coasts (see Fig. 1.3), ~~they~~have been used
by people in many ways for thousands of years. ~~They are found in large~~
~~numbers at low tide level, as seen in the picture below.~~ Many seaweeds are
rich in iodine and can be used as food for grazing animals, such as sheep.
Some kinds are also used as food for people, and others are processed to produce chemicals that give bulk ~~to~~and a smooth texture to factory-made foods
such as ice cream. ~~Burned~~When burned, seaweeds yield a fine ash that is
rich in potassium salts ~~which~~and is used as ~~is~~ a chemical fertilizer. The best
seaweeds for making fertilizer are the kelps, some of which are ~~really~~very
large. One species, the Giant Kelp, grows deep ~~down~~in the Atlantic Ocean,
sometimes as much as 30 ~~thirty meters~~metres ~~deep~~below the water's surface. This species can produce a repeatedly branched stem up to 174 metres
long~~. Thus~~, making it ~~is~~one of the largest plants in the world.

Seaweeds are simple, usually feathery or ribbon-like plants that have no systems of veins and no roots, leaves or woody parts. Instead of a root, many of
them have a special organ called a holdfast, which enables the seaweed to
remain anchored to rocks during the roughest seas (see Fig. 1.4). If the holdfast breaks away from the rock, the seaweed will drift away and die. Some
species do not have a holdfast and live by floating through the water.

Most seaweeds reproduce sexually. This is a fairly simple process, ~~but~~
although it varies in detail from one species to another.~~in detail.~~ Special cells
in the body of the seaweed produce male and female cells. These cells can be
very simple and superficially identical with other, ordinary body cells.~~In,~~ but
in some species they are larger and more complex. As in other types of
plants, the female cell is ~~fertilised~~fertilized by the male and the result is the
formation of an embryo, which soon develops into another plant. In those
seaweeds that do not reproduce sexually, new plants grow from fragments
that are detached from the body of the plant.

~~Seaweeds are simple, usually feathery or ribbon-like plants that have no sys-~~
~~tems of veins and no roots, leaves or woody parts. Instead of a root, many of~~
~~them have a special organ called a holdfast which enables the seaweed to~~
~~remain anchored to rocks during the roughest seas (see diagram below). If~~
~~the holdfast breaks away from the rock, the seaweed will drift away and die.~~
~~Some species do not have a holdfast and live by floating through the water.~~
~~One of these free-floaters is Sargassum natans. It does not reproduce sexually:~~
~~new plants grow from fragment s that are detached from the body of the~~
~~plant.~~

~~The Algae:~~@B: ~~f~~Freshwater and terrestrial

Most algae are much smaller than seaweeds ~~and~~ indeed, many of them are among the world's smallest green plants. Many algae are single-celled and often exist as individual plants, although some of them live in groups. Others ~~algae~~ are threads of cells and form thick hair-like mats in ponds and lakes.

The majority of the single-celled species live in the sea, usually in the upper layers. ~~There,~~ where they form an important part of plankton, ~~the drifting mass of minute plant and animal life that is so important as a food for many specie of fish~~. The algae in the plankton are called phytoplankton and are the starting point of all marine food chains.

Many other single-celled algae live in fresh water, such as those that form the familiar scum on ponds. A few single-celled species live on land. For example, there is one species that lives on tree trunks, wooden fences, brick and stone of all types, ~~forms~~ forming a greyish-green powder when dry and a bright green one when damp ~~on tree trunks, wooden fences, brick and stone of all types~~(see Fig. 1.5). ~~, as shown in the photo below.~~

These freshwater, marine and terrestrial algae are classified into five main divisions. Members of the many families of the Chlorophyta division range from single-celled land forms to large seaweeds. All species make carbohydrates from carbon dioxide and water by photosynthesis and are among the most important producers of food for animals. They are colonizers of suitable habitats and, as they can reproduce both sexually and asexually very rapidly, they can exist in enormous quantities, with tens of thousands of individuals of one species closely packed together.

The Euglenophyta algae are very unusual in that most of them have also been claimed ~~by zoologists~~ as animals by zoologists! This is for three reasons. Firstly, they can ~~move~~ move: ~~because~~ they have one or more whiplike flagellae, which they use to propel themselves through the water in which they live. Of course, bacteria can do this too, so it is not a good enough reason by itself. Secondly, many of them can eat solid foods. ~~they have a llkight sensitive red eye spot which enables them to seek out the light so that they can photosynthesize at the fastest possible rate.~~ Thirdly, they have a light-sensitive red eye spot, which enables them to seek out the light so that they can photosynthesize at the fastest possible rate.~~many of them can eat solid foods.~~ However, it is precisely because the Euglenophyta produce food by photosynthesis, like other green plants, that most scientists consider them to be plants. ~~(but see Peterson, 1999).~~ Several species produce very thick-walled cysts, which are a prolonged resting place. This mechanism for remaining inactive also indicates that they are plants rather than animals.

~~The members~~Most species of the Pyrrophyta division, like ~~are similar to~~ those of the Eulenophyta, ~~in that most species~~have flagella and possibly take in solid food. ~~They differ from~~Unlike ~~them~~the Eulenophyta, ~~in that~~their ~~colouring~~pigments are not typically grass-green but vary from ~~yellowish~~ yellowish-green to golden-brown. Most species are single-celled and some, such as *Dinamoebideum varians*, are very similar to animals like the amoeba. Another group have their cells joining end to end to form branching threads.

The Cyanophyta algae usually have a blue ~~colouring~~pigment that can mask the green chlorophyll. This is why they are called the blue-green algae. This is the only division ~~is unique in that~~in which sexual reproduction has never been observed. All ~~multiplication~~reproduction takes place by cell division. The resulting offspring usually stay together to form threads or a colony held together in a jelly-like envelope. Some species can move by sliding along on a slime they produce.

Most species live in fresh water but some grow on damp rocks, others in and on soil as colonizers and a few grow in the outflow from hot springs. These thermal algae, as they are called, can ~~even multiply~~reproduce in temperatures as high as 75 °~~degrees Celsius~~. ~~It has been suggested that they were~~They may have been among the first plants in the world ~~and, lived~~ living in the hot waters that were much more widespread when the ~~earth~~ Earth first started to cool down.

The ~~six thousand~~6000 species of the Chrysophyta division include the yellow-green algae, the ~~golden~~golden-brown algae and the diatoms (see page ~~43~~XX). The yellow-green and golden-brown species can be solitary or united in colonies. They live in the sea, in fresh water and in damp spots, where they ~~are~~often intermingles with mosses, liverworts and other kinds of algae.

~~The Algae~~@B: ~~d~~Diatoms

Diatoms, ~~meaning two atoms,~~are minute single-celled plants that grow in water. Their most characteristic feature ~~of the diatoms~~is that the outer layer, or wall, of each cell is impregnated with a hard mineral called silica. This gives each species a very distinct appearance when viewed through a microscope, which is the only way to see them. ~~They come in many shapes and sizes~~ (see ~~photo below~~Fig. 1.6). The stiffened cell wall is like a box in two almost equal parts ~~side by side~~that overlap. This is why these algae are called diatoms, meaning two atoms. The silica ~~cell~~walls remain when the living

~~algae~~plant inside dies and decays, and ~~they~~can become preserved in the deposi~~tions~~ that form at the bottom of the pond or sea in which ~~they~~it lived.

Nearly 6000 species of diatom are known. The many living species are an important source of food to fish and animals. However, some of the diatoms are known only as fossils. Where conditions for diatom growth were extremely favourable in the ~~passed~~past, such as when the seas were still very warm, vast deposits of diatom fossils were ~~also~~also formed. Many of these 'diatomaceous earth' rocks lie close to deposits of oil. ~~It is widely agreed that it could be~~Scientists believe that oil ~~was~~may have been formed from plants that were very similar to diatoms but did not have the rigid silica walls. ~~In the Santa Maria oil fields in California deposits of fossilised diatoms over 1000 metres deep have been discovered.~~

@A:~~The Fungi~~Fungi~~: moulds and yeasts~~
~~Moulds, like those that grow on stale bread, are one of the many species of fungi.~~Fungi (the plural of fungus) are simple plants that, like algae, are not divided into roots, stems and leaves, but have a body. The body consists of very fine branching threads, called hyphae, that are actively feeding and growing. They form a network, rather like a cobweb, over and in the food on which they live.

@B:Moulds and yeasts
Moulds, like those that grow on stale bread, are one of the many species of fungi. Some moulds are harmful and destructive. They can grow on food and fabrics, live on petrol and reduce its ability to drive engines, attack paint and even destroy stonework and bricks. Some moulds are useful. They are used as flavourings in blue-veined cheeses and are processed to make some antibiotics.

The editor has done a good job, but made one mistake in house style. Before you ask the editor to revise all the four-digit numbers, consider how much of the job has been completed and how important the correction is. If only a small amount of text has been edited, then asking for this correction to be made is a good idea: it reminds the copy-editor to review and be careful about the house style. However, if a large proportion of the material has been edited, you might decide that because this particular element of house style is of relatively minor importance and has been imposed consistently, although incorrectly, it will not affect the saleability of the book and can be left as is, although you will tell the copy-editor to be more careful in future. But if the book is one of a series, then it would be essential to correct the error now rather than perpetuate it and make the series inconsistent or confuse other copy-editors who might work on the series.

The copy-editor also made an error in presentation: the text should be unjustified. You can easily correct this before sending the files to the next stage; again, tell the copy-editor to be sure to do this in future.

Some mistakes are more serious even on a single title. For example, neglecting to impose the -ize spelling could affect the sales in markets where that is the only spelling used; leaving location references to illustrations, unless instructed, would create extra work at page proof; and leaving cross-references to pre-typeset folios could cause confusion, particularly if they are not corrected at proof. Getting the copy-editor to correct these errors is essential; doing so at an early stage in the project means that the remedial work should not affect the schedule.

Anyone can – and everyone does – make mistakes, and minor errors can be corrected, but restructuring, rewriting or even basic editing that is detrimental to the original requires more drastic action. Do not panic. Instead:

* analyse what is wrong;
* check that the brief is clear;
* discuss the problems with the copy-editor.

Can the copy-editor offer a convincing reason for what has happened? For example, can he or she show that the brief was ambiguous and that his or her misinterpretation was reasonable, or that the original or edited e-files were corrupted? If so, return the work for revision and check again soon.

Being tired or ill or having domestic problems may well elicit your sympathy but are not reasons you can afford to accept. Problems like these are likely to continue or recur, and the editor should have been more vigilant about the work because of them. He or she could also have contacted you about the schedule if extending it would have overcome a temporary problem. Defending the quality of bad work is a clear indication that this copy-editor is not appropriate for the job. You need to stop the work immediately and work out a fair compensation for what has been done. When the contract for the services stipulates an hourly rate, you have to pay for the time spent. If, however, the agreement is for a fee, you are entitled to take into account the unacceptable standard of work in determining a cancellation fee.

Replacing the copy-editor – or any other individual whose work is below par – is a top priority. Again, don't panic. Find another copy-editor. This time you will be looking for someone who, in addition to having the other qualities the job requires, can work to a tight schedule. Do not let the pressure of the schedule tempt you into trying to persuade someone to take on the work if they are doubtful about completing it on time; that can lead to even worse problems. Find someone who can either assure you of completing by the original scheduled date or knows it isn't possible and offers an alternative date. In the latter instance, consider the alternative date and discuss it with the commissioning editor, design manager and production manager. Perhaps the publication date can be saved. If not, it may be better to revise the schedule and produce the right quality product than to publish a substandard product on time.

Proofreading

Unless the proofs are read and returned in batches, you check them only when the proofreading is complete. Thus the importance of choosing an appropriate, competent and reliable proofreader and providing a clear and accurate brief is very clear.

Remember that, as with copy-editing, you are checking, not doing. Divide the task into parts and focus on each one in turn.

1 Read your brief and check examples of specific points listed there.
2 Check that the standard symbols have been used, and that they are marked correctly and clearly in the text and in the margins.
3 Spot-check that the colours have been used accurately, then look at the proportion of red and blue. A lot of red corrections can indicate poor typesetting, areas of incompatibility between the word processing and typesetting systems or, if the copy-editor supplied edited e-files, poor keyboarding or file preparation by that person.

A lot of blue corrections might indicate that the editing was of a poorer quality than you thought; in that case, analyse the copy-editor's shortcomings, work out the effect on the budget and use the information in your feedback. Alternatively, a lot of blue on the proofs might indicate that the proofreader is making unnecessary or wrong changes. Determine which it is and use the information in your feedback later, but right now decide the most efficient way of correcting the proofreader's work. When you have arranged that the copy-editor will collate these proofs with those of the author, all you have to do is brief him or her to reject all unnecessary changes. If you had originally decided to do the collation yourself, consider whether in these circumstances you can do it as quickly as the copy-editor, who knows the material better, or whether the time and budget will allow for the copy-editor to do it instead.

4 Look at the queries. Are they concise, clear, circled and removable, and reasonable? Reasonable queries seek to clarify ambiguities, for example, or point out repetitions, contradictions, inconsistencies or unintentional omissions. Unreasonable queries concern basic spelling, word breaks or grammar, all of which the proofreader can check in reference books.

5 Are there any messages to the designer or typesetter? They should be in red and circled, and as concise as clarity allows. These notes might key in illustrations, indicate corrections to the orientation or location of illustrations or mark corrections to typesetting styles. See what they tell you about the work done by the designer or typesetter, and use this information later in feedback.

6 Skim the proofs to check that references to pages 00 or XX have been replaced with numbers or been highlighted if it is to be done at a later stage. Is the colour used the one stipulated in your brief?

7 Read a few random paragraphs that have not been marked for correction to make sure the proofreader has been accurate.

Exercise 6.3: Checking the proofreader's work

The original copy was sent to the typesetter as an e-file with hard-copy mark-up. Here are the page proofs read by the proofreader. The proofreader was briefed to:

* use blue (shown as Ⓑ) for inserting cross-referenced pages;
* use red (other marks) to key in figures in boxed areas;
* be aware that attributes may have been lost when transferring material from the word-processing program to the typesetting program and to mark resulting corrections in red.

Assess the proofreader's work and note what it tells you about work done at earlier stages.

---

14 Destructive margin processes

Geological and geophysical characteristics

The Earth's crust has formed from the mantle as a result of magmatic activity over at least 3800 million years (Ma). At present such activity occurs dominantly at lithospheric plate boundaries and to a minor degree within plates. Volcanism at constructive margins (oceanic ridges) is dominantly submarine and basaltic, with the products forming the oceanic crust. Destructive plate boundaries form island arcs an active continental margins, where the volcanic products range from basalt through andesite and dacite to rhyolite. This chapter describes processes active at destructive plate margins and those involved in collisions between island arcs and continents, and between continents, i.e. the processes forming orogenic belts.

The advent of the theory of plate tectonics (see Chapter 10) during the 1960s led to a reappraisal of processes in orogenic zones. Before the plate tectonics era orogenic activity was considered to conform to a broad pattern or cycle, the earliest stage of which was the eruption of basaltic lavas (spilites) within a flysch-type sedimentary sequence deposited in a linear belt or geosyncline along a continual margin. Then, during the early stages of deformation of the sedimentary-volcanic succession, ultrabasic and basic intrusions were emplaced. The third stage, during and after the main episode of deformation, was the intrusion of batholiths of diorite-granodiorite-granite composition. Finally, following elevation of the folded sedimentary-volcanic pile, volcanic rocks of the orogenic andesite association were erupted.

Before the concept of plate tectonics, the major problem was to explain this orogenic cycle. It was assumed that the geosynclinal belts evolved in depressions in the continental crust, possibly located over sinking mantle convection currents. It then followed that deformation could occur when the continental crust below the depression melted and became less rigid, allowing the sedimentary-volcanic pile to be compressed and deformed. When sinking ceased, uplift of the deformed orgenic belt occurred and melting in the mantle or at the base of the thickened pile led to the formation of magmas that were intruded

or erupted at the surface. Plate tectonic processes provide an alternative to this 'ensialic' model of the orogenic cycle.

Island arcs, active continental margins and collision zones have been abundant throughout much of geological time. At present most of these features are located around the Pacific (see page XXX). The western Pacific has major arcs extending from the New Zealand–Tonga system through New Britain–Papua New Guinea and the Mariana–Volcano Islands, to the Japanese Kuril–Kamchatka system. The Mariana–Volcano system and the Japanese arc are separated from the continent by 'marginal' basins formed, similarly to larger ocean basins, by sea-floor spreading. Thus the Sea of Japan formed as a result of subduction below the Japanese landmass, which caused melting in the mantle and splitting away of the Japanese islands from the Asian mainland. Such splitting explains the origin of marginal or 'back-arc' basins as a result of orogenic processes. Such back-arc basins occur behind the Kamchatka–Kuril arcs (Sea of Okhotsk), the Japanese arc (Sea of Japan), the Philippines (the Philippine Sea) and Taiwan (East China Sea). As these marginal seas have increased in area the arcuate forms of the island arcs bounding them have become more pronounced. Formation of a back-arc basin might split the island arc off an inactive arc on the continent side of the basin and the active arc. Such 'bending' of the eastern Pacific island arcs is a result of the process of back-arc spreading. With the exception of Japan, these arcs appear to lack ancient continental basement.

In contrast to the western Pacific the eastern Pacific has no island arcs but has volcanism on an active continental margin extending from the western USA, through Mexico and Central America, to the western margin of South America. A similar situation exists along the Indonesian margins of south-east Asia, but here the continent is largely submarine. In the Atlantic, the Lesser Antilles and the South Sandwich Islands are young arcs associated with marginal basins. The characteristics of the basins behind the Mediterranean Aeolian and Aegean arcs are, however, more ambiguous. The most extensive active continental collision zone extends from the Alps through Turkey and Iran to the Himalayas.

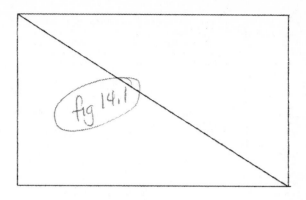

14.1 *Landsat image of Subawa Island in the Indonesian island arc. The Tombora volcano, which gave the largest historic eruption in Indonesia, in 1815, is at the top.*

Some of the major geological and geophysical characteristics of volcanic arcs and active continental margins were described in Chapter 10. The major features are summarized below.

1 Arcuate distribution of islands, or a linear belt of volcanism, with a length of the order of several thousands of kilometres and a relatively narrow width. In many arcs, particularly where they are split by back-arc spreading, the area on the oceanic side of the volcanic belt consists of an outer arc region and an accretionary wedge or subduction complex extending to the trench.

2 A trench on the oceanic side, often between 6000 and 11,000 m deep, and (behind island arcs) a shallow tray-shaped marginal basin sea on the continental side, generally less than 3000 m deep.

3 Active volcanism, with an abrupt oceanward boundary of the volcanic zone parallel to, and about 200 km from, the oceanic trench. This is known as the volcanic front. The concentration of volcanoes is greatest here and decreases with increasing distance from the trench.

4 Active seismicity, including shallow, intermediate and deep earthquakes, extending as a well-defined plane from below the trench towards the marginal basin or continental side. Compared with the mantle below the island arc, that below the marginal basin has low seismic velocities and high attenuation of seismic waves.

5 A marked gravity anomaly belt: a negative anomaly of up to 100 milligals is associated with the trench; positive anomalies occur on the arc or continental margin.

6 A marked heat-flow anomaly belt: heat flow is relatively low in the trench area (generally <40 mW/m²) and higher at the island arc or continental margin (>40 mW/m²).

7 In some island arcs, notably Japan, there is a distinct zonal arrangement in the composition of volcanic rocks. Volcanoes near the volcanic front erupt tholeiitic basalts, while volcanoes farther away erupt more alkaline basalts. In many, but not all, island arcs and active continental margins the potassium content at a given silica percentage increases towards the back of the arc.

The characteristics of volcanic arcs and active continental margins summarized above may be explained in terms of plate tectonics. Cold, dense lithosphere sinks into the mantle from the oceanic trench along a seismic plane termed the Benioff, or subduction, zone. This explains the negative gravity anomalies and low heat flow associated with oceanic trenches. At a particular depth the descending slab melts or dehydrates, releasing volatiles into the overlying mantle wedge, thus causing melting, rise and intrusion of magma and surface volcanism. More extensive island/arc orogenesis may lead to more extensive melting and the formation of a marginal basin. The formation of island arcs as outlined above has been termed island-arc-type orogeny.

Island/arc orogeny
The sequence of events in the formation of a single volcanic arc may be as follows. The development of a trench may be associated with initiation of plate descent, and simultaneously there may be complex thrusting of wedge-shaped slices of oceanic crust and mantle. During early thrusting, oceanic sediments (including cherts, argillites and carbonates)

may slide into the trench by gravity. Such slides may carry blocks of basic and ultrabasic rocks derived from disrupted, faulted and thrust blocks.

The slide deposit may be carried into a deformed sedimentary accretionary wedge beneath and behind the trench. This wedge, a complex mixture, or melange, of varied sedimentary and igneous rocks scraped from the descending plate, may experience strong deformation and metamorphism within the blueschist facies (low temperature-high pressure) in the low heat flow regimes of the trench. Such subduction complexes occur in many western Pacific volcanic arcs.

The evolution of the accretionary prism depends upon the way in which sedimentary material is scraped off the oceanic plate descending below the island arc. Where a thick sediment cover overlies the oceanic plate entering the subduction zone (e.g. as a result of proximity to a continental landmass) pockets of sediment are sequentially scraped off the descending plate, since they are much less dense than the oceanic lithosphere. When the process occurs for a prolonged period of time, an accretionary prism is built up in the outer arc region. The accretionary prism consists of a sequence of layers of sedimentary rocks emplaced above the descending oceanic plate. Each layer may show a sequence from ophiolitic ocean floor rocks, through cherts and/or argillites up into flysch sediments. Hence the beds within each layer get younger towards the island arc, but the sequence of layers as a whole (youngs) towards the ocean. In active island arcs the breaks between the sediment layers are manifested as regularly spaced, large fault planes. These are initially low-angle fault planes but rotate to a high angle as the accretionary prism builds up. Prolonged accretion

then gives rise to a ridge feature: the trench-slope break forms the outer arc terrain, separating a relatively undeformed upper slope basin between the volcanic arc and the break, and the accretionary prism between the break and the trench. Generally, the trench-slope break is below sea level in active arcs, but in some cases (eg in Alaska, see page XXX) parts are emergent and form islands composed of layers of trench sediments separated by the characteristic faulting.

When the descending plate capped with hydrated oceanic crust and/or some oceanic sediment reaches a depth of about 100 km, dehydration releases hydrous fluids into the overlying mantle wedge. This initiates melting, and the parent magmas for the igneous rocks of the volcanic arc are formed. At or following this stage the arc may become split by back-arc spreading, as described earlier. In the volcanic arc the rocks are of basic and intermediate composition: gabbro and diorite intrusions are emplaced into the crust, and a volcanic pile of basalt and basaltic andesite begins to accumulate at the surface.

Where continued magmatic activity heats and thins the lithosphere, high temperature–high pressure metamorphism of the crust occurs. The crust thickens by intrusion and growth of the volcanic pile, together with continued deformation and accretion. Migration of the igneous axis may occur, yielding inner and outer arcs. During crustal growth an oceanward thickening wedge of flysch sediment, derived from the volcanic belt, develops between the active volcanic front and the trench. At this stage a volcanic arc with paired metamorphic zonation (low temperature–high pressure near the trench, high temperature/low pressure near the active axis) may be developed.

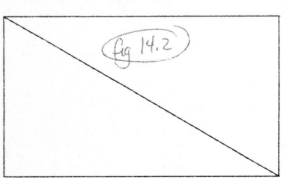

14.2 Block diagram of a typical subduction zone of island/arc type, showing the various subdivisions of and arc system and the structural complexity of the subducted sediments.

Clearly, therefore, oceanic trenches and their associated sedimentary wedges are likely to be extremely complicated terrains, with complex geometric and time relationships between varied components of the oceanic crust and upper mantle, melange, intrusive and volcanic rocks and derived flysch sediments.

Cordilleran belts

In contrast to the island-arc-type orogeny described above, the orogenic belts of the eastern Pacific occur not as island arcs but along continental margins. These are cordilleran-type orogenic belts. Such a situation may originate where an inactive Atlantic-type continental margin becomes active by development of a trench. During and after the formation of a destructive margin near the continental margin, the sequence of events within and behind the newly formed trench may be similar to that described above for island arcs. However, the presence of continental crust provides additional complexities. For example, the sedimentary rocks formed before initiation of the trench may include continental shelf carbonates and continental rise argillites and clastic rocks. The sequence of events may include formation of blue schist melanges and flysch accumulations.

When the subducted oceanic lithosphere reaches depths of about 100 km, dehydration and possibly melting of the descending oceanic crust occurs. The resulting magmas rise, intrusions may thus be emplaced and submarine volcanic rocks may be erupted near the volcanic front. As in island arcs, these igneous rocks are relatively basic in composition and include diorites with basalts and basaltic andesite. The igneous axis may migrate towards the continent and then encroach upon older crust. This leads to underplating and intrusion, and therefore to thickening of the continental crust. Uplift will cause subsequent volcanism to be subaerial. At this stage the intrusive rocks belong to the diorite–granodiorite–granite association, and erupted rocks are andesite and dacite lavas and pyroclastic rocks (air-fall and pyroclastic flows, including ignimbrites) containing dacite and rhyolite. Formation of these rocks may involve melting of old continental basement. The intrusive and extrusive rocks may show a compositional polarity analogous to that described for island arcs. The subaerial volcanic belt forms an axis from which sediments are eroded and then transported both into the trench and towards the continent. Subsequent evolution may be dominated by thrusting towards the continental side of the magmatic axis, involving the flysch and sometimes the continental basement.

Active orogenic belts have a range of characteristics between cordilleran- and island-arc-type belts. Complex orogenic belts develop from collision of an island arc with either an Atlantic-type continental margin or a cordilleran-type orogenic belt. A further complexity arises from the direction of subduction below the arc; subduction might be oblique to the trench of the arc or might pass into strike-slip faults that traverse some island arcs (e.g. Sumatra) and cordilleran margins (e.g. New

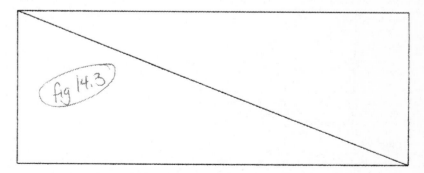

14.3 Destructive plate margin of cordilleran type. Subduction of oceanic crust along a trench gives rise to mountain building and intrusive and extrusive igneous activity within the continent.

Zealand). In addition multiple collisions of island arcs as a result of subduction processes or strike-slip faulting may lead to formation of larger continental masses with complex structural characteristics.

Continental collision zones

The most complex situation develops where two continental blocks approach and collide by subduction of the intervening oceanic crust. Such a collision is believed to be responsible for formation of the Alpine–Himalayan orogenic belt. In the simplest case, we may consider the approach of an Atlantic-type continental margin to another continent bounded by a cordilleran-type orogenic belt. As the Atlantic-type margin meets the trench there may be deformation and thrusting of the continental basement, and nappes may eventually form. Oceanic crust, upper mantle, oceanic sediments and flysch deposits are deformed and thrust over earlier thrust-sheets. When the collision is arrested by the buoyancy of the collided continental masses, the collision zone becomes an area of thickened crust characterized by complex faulting, including prominent lateral faulting, and uplift.

The structures developed during collision between continents depend upon the natures of the sedimentary sequence and the basement on the Atlantic-type margin, and the shapes of the colliding margins. Where margins are irregular, the first continental segments to collide will experience the earliest and most intense deformation. Such segments may be partially subducted or split, so that the upper part becomes 'flaked' onto the continent. Alternatively, the segments may be extended by lateral faulting, and as a result generate a more even collision. Against such regions the trench zone becomes a narrow suture from which fragments of oceanic crust, mantle, oceanic sediments and flysch sediments are transported. These regions are likely to have extensive continentally derived molasse sediments in external troughs. In contrast to collided segments, some portions of incidental areas of the continental margins may never collide, so that relatively undeformed areas of oceanic crust are preserved within the orogenic belt.

Continent/continent collision zones are clearly likely to be extremely complex. Before collision the ocean may include small island arcs and small continental masses. At the initiation of collision the margins may split, forming a complex pattern of small continental fragments that eventually become sutured along the collision zone.

Petrological characteristics
Volcanic rocks
Whereas the volcanic rocks erupted along the destructive margins can be relatively easily collected and studied, this is not true of the intrusive rocks believed to be present below the volcanic belt. Because such intrusive rocks are exposed by erosion in areas of active or geologically recent subduction, they are widely believed to represent magmas that have crystallized below an overlying contemporaneous volcanic belt. However, this is very difficult to prove. Furthermore, there are likely to be differences between the compositions of contemporaneous extrusive and intrusive rocks, reflecting their contrasted occurrence and cooling environment. Nevertheless, the mineral and chemical compositions of extrusive and intrusive rocks emplaced at destructive margins show clear parallels.

As already explained, the igneous rocks of destructive margins range from basic to acid in chemical composition: the intrusive rocks for the gabbro–diorite–granodiorite–granite association and the volcanic rocks form the basalt–andesite–dacite–rhyolite association. There is continuous mineralogical variation within these series, as shown in Figure 5.17. The basic rocks are composed of Ca-rich plagioclase, pyroxenes and/or amphiboles with minor olivine and Fe–Ti oxide, and grade through intermediate rocks, composed largely of intermediate plagioclase with pyroxenes and/or amphiboles and quartz, to acid rocks composed largely of Na-rich plagioclase, alkali feldspar and quartz. These mineralogical variations are paralleled by continuous chemical variations, as shown on a plot of element oxides against silica (SiO_2) in Figure 14.4.

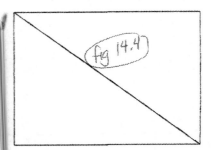

14.4 Chemical variation diagram showing proportions of important elements (as their oxides) against percentage of silica (i.e. acidity).

14.5: Representative chemical analyses of volcanic and intrusive rocks from destructive plate margins.

	1	2	3	4	5	6	7	8
SiO_2	50.3	62.5	67.4	74.2	48.3	59.1	66.2	75.3
TiO_2	21.0	0.6	0.7	0.3	0.6	0.6	0.6	0.2
Al_2O_3	20.3	15.9	15.3	13.3	19.1	17.1	15.5	12.9
Fe_2O_3	3.0	1.3	3.6	0.9	2.8	2.4	1.7	0.3
FeO	5.5	3.3	1.1	0.9	7.0	5.0	2.6	0.8
MnO	0.2	0.1	0.1	0.1	0.2	0.2	0.1	0.1
MgO	4.3	3.5	1.0	0.3	8.0	2.7	1.8	0.4
CaO	11.0	4.6	3.4	1.6	11.2	5.7	3.1	0.8
Na_2O	3.3	4.2	4.6	4.2	2.0	3.1	2.8	3.9
K_2O	0.4	2.8	2.4	3.2	0.2	2.6.	4.4	4.4
P_2O_5	0.1	0.2	0.2	0.1	0.1	0.2	0.1	
H_2O	0.7	1.8	0.8	1.0				
Total	100.1	100.8	100.6	100.1	99.5	98.7	98.9	99.1

Notes to columns terms in parentheses refer to the classification of volcanic rocks as shown in Figure 14.6).
1 Basalt (low-K tholeiite), Mt Misery volcano, St Kitts, Lesser Antilles.
2 Andesite (high-K andesite), San Pedrovolcano, north Chile.
3 Dacite (dacite), Maungaongaonga, New Zealand.
4 Rhyolite (average of twenty-five analyses), New Zealand.
5 Gabbro (average of eight analyses), Peruvian coastal batholith.
6 Diorite, Linga su per unit, Arequipa segment of Peruvian coastal batholith.
7 Granodiorite, Linga su per unit, Arequipa segment of Peruvian coastal batholith.
8 Granite, Parivilca pluton, Lima segment of Peruvian coastal batholith.

From basic to acid compositions there is a decrease in total FeO, MgO and CaO, and an increase in Na_2O and K_2O. Chemical analyses of representative intrusive and extrusive rocks are given in Figure 14.5.

The volcanic rocks show a progressive increase in K_2O relative to SiO_2 from the trench towards the island arc or continent. The volcanic associations may therefore be further subdivided on a plot of K_2O against SiO_2. Although variation is continuous, certain distinctive associations may be recognized and these are low-K, calc-alkaline, high-K and shoshonitic associations. Volcanic rocks of the low-K association have tholeiitic characteristics and are often termed the island-arc tholeiite series. This, like other tholeiitic series, shows a trend of enrichment of total FeO relative to MgO in a diagram showing relative variations in $Na_2O + K_2O$ (alkalis), total FeO (FeO) and MgO (an AFM diagram). By contrast, the calc-alkaline association does not show such Fe enrichment. The tholeiitic association is dominated by basalts and basaltic andesites, while the calc-alkaline association has greater amounts of andesites. The characteristics of island arc tholeiitic and calc-alkaline associations are summarized in Figure 14.10. It is important to note that there is complete gradation from the island arc tholeiitic series, through low-K, calc-alkaline, to the calc-alkaline association.

The western Pacific island arcs appear to show evolutionary sequence of island-arc volcanism. Relatively young ones, such as the Mariana and Tonga–Kermadec arcs and the South Sandwich arc in the south Atlantic, while exhibiting a complete spectrum of volcanic rocks, from basalt to rhyolite, are dominantly composed of basalt and basaltic andesite of the island arc tholeiitic association. Older and hence more evolved arcs such as Japan, Indonesia, Kamchatka and the Aleutians, and continental margins like the Cascades in north-west USA and the central Andes, have a similar range of composition but consist dominantly of calc-alkaline andesites. In some evolved arcs, such as Indonesia, and continental margins, such as the central Andes, high-K calc-alkaline and shoshonitic volcanic rocks are erupted. Thus the lower parts of evolved island arcs consist of tholeiitic rocks, while the upper parts comprise calc-alkaline and shoshonitic volcanic rocks. There is, therefore, a compositional stratification in an evolved island arc, the upper part being richer in SiO_2, K_2O and associated trace elements, and having a lower FeO/MgO ratio, because of the stratigraphic variations described above.

Increase in K_2O with distance from the oceanic trench at a given SiO_2 content was first demonstrated in the Japanese arc where tholeiitic volcanic rocks occur near the trench, fol-

lowed inland by calc-alkaline and alkaline volcanic rocks. This compositional trend has
been demonstrated in many arcs, Indonesia
for example, and continental margins (the
central Andes), but is not found everywhere.
Since the major chemical variation is in the
K_2O content at given SiO_2, and since this cor-
relates with depth to the Benioff zone (h), it is
known as the K–h relationship.

Intrusive rocks

The chemical characteristics and the compositional variations with space and time outlined for volcanic rocks above also characterize
intrusive rocks of destructive margins.
However, the relationship of extrusive and
intrusive rocks is not unequivocal: young
intrusive rocks are not yet exposed by erosion,

and exposed intrusions may not represent
magmatic liquid compositions or may be
hydrothermally altered because of slow cooling in the presence of meteoric water.
Intrusive rocks emplaced at destructive margins and continent–continent collision zones
have a broad spectrum of basic to acid chemical compositions. Intrusive associations are
referred to as igneous, or I-type, granites and
sedimentary, or S-type, granites, these being
end-members of a spectrum of granite types.
The characteristics of I- and S-type granites
(Figure 14.13) probably indicate a fundamen-
tal difference between the source regions
referred to in their names. Both I- and S-type
granites occur in distinctive tectonic environ-
ments, which are described later.

The proofreader has followed the brief and done a good job. The
fact that quite a few of the red corrections – hyphens for rules, lower-
case instead of subscript numerals – could be attributed to program
incompatibilities should lead you to discuss with the design and production managers whether there are better ways to present material
electronically to avoid such problems.

Analysing the nature of the blue corrections and seeing that the
copy-editor has made the same error several times would lead you
first to check more of the proofs to see whether this cluster was
unique or part of a larger pattern. In the former case it would be sufficient simply to remark on the error; in the latter, it would be
necessary to remind the copy-editor that maintaining consistency is a
basic competence and that keeping a style sheet can help to do this.

One of the queries shows that the copy-editor has also overlooked
the fact that the information in the note to the columns is inconsistent
with the table. Again, if this is a unique error, point out how serious
it could have been if the proofreader hadn't caught it; if there are
many such apparent oversights, ask the copy-editor for an explanation, emphasize the quality of work expected and make a note for
yourself to check these aspects of the copy-editor's task more carefully
if you work together in the future.

It won't have taken you long to reach these conclusions if you looked
at and thought about the corrections and queries in an organized way.

Picture research

As stated earlier, there are usually two picture meetings. You decide who should attend these meetings in addition to yourself and the picture researcher. Depending on the nature of the project, other appropriate personnel would be the author(s) or the general editor, the copy-editor, and the designer. As project manager you might have the final say in which images are selected, so it is very important that you listen carefully to the opinions of the others. Images are selected on the basis of:

1 Editorial content
2 Visual impact
3 Reproduction quality

Authors and copy-editors will put more emphasis on point 1, and designers on points 2 and 3. Picture researchers are concerned with point 1 to the extent that they must get images of the subjects listed; those given a copy of the text have the opportunity to be more precise about the editorial content of the images they pre-select.

At preliminary selection meetings picture researchers should bring a number of images for each subject on the list, unless the subjects are so specific that only one image is possible. You expect them to have pre-selected these images from all that they have collected, returning those that don't fulfil all of the criteria above or skipping over them on a CD. At the meeting a smaller selection may be made for use by the designer. Sometimes none of the images for a subject is adequate and so gaps are identified, to be filled by the final selection date.

To assess the quality of the picture researcher's work, consider:

* what percentage of the subjects have been covered;
* the extent to which specific elements of the brief have been followed – for example, providing not only the right subjects but also the views requested, or new or little-used images;
* whether any of the images should have been discarded in pre-selection because of damage, poor visual impact or poor reproduction quality.

While checking on the schedule should ensure that there are enough images available to make the meeting worth having, it might still be that an insufficient number of subjects has been covered. Remember that the time between preliminary selection and final selection is intended for filling gaps identified at the earlier meeting and obtaining originals for reproduction when copies have been used for selection purposes, not for doing the basic research. When the majority of subjects is not covered at the first meeting, find out why: has the researcher not put in enough time, not gone to appropriate sources, or not chased sources to deliver? Then give the picture researcher specific instructions on what to do and when to do it – do not expect generalities like 'Put in more time' and 'We need to see more pictures quickly' to overcome these problems – and set a date for another meeting at which you expect to see the majority of the subjects.

Reread the brief and take it with you to the meeting. Although you will be considering the quality of the images, you are judging the picture researcher's work partly on the extent to which those images fulfil the brief. Whenever a picture is of the wrong subject or not the view requested, look at the brief with the researcher, and with the copy-editor if you have delegated the briefing. If the brief is at fault, admit it, revise it and make sure that it is now accurate, unambiguous, and as precise as necessary. When the brief is not the cause of the problem, discuss the reasons with the picture researcher. A mistake here and there might be the result of a misreading or a misunderstanding, but a significant number of errors points in the direction of carelessness or incompetence. In this case, again, give specific instructions to remedy the situation and arrange another meeting with just you and the researcher to check progress.

Picture researchers are justified in bringing pictures of poor reproduction quality to a meeting for only three reasons:
• to assess editorial content prior to obtaining a better original
• because that is all the budget allows
• because it is the only image of the subject
Otherwise, tell researchers who select such pictures to make the group for selection larger; they are wasting everyone's valuable time and energy. Tell those who don't pre-select to do so, for the same reason. And tell those who cannot distinguish quality to get some more training, because this is an essential skill, a mark of competence.

Since you've had interim meetings where necessary to make sure picture researchers solved any problems identified earlier, the final selection meeting should go well. Later, you will also assess the quality of the researcher's work on other aspects of the brief: the preparation of the acknowledgements, the negotiation of rights within budget, the return of used materials where required, and the handover of the documentation. In all these cases you are looking for accuracy in every detail, clarity, good organization and, of course, punctuality.

Index

The only opportunity to check the quality of the indexer's work is when it is done. You can ask the copy-editor to edit it and then look at the results, or you can edit it yourself. As always, break the job down into separate elements (see page 82) and check them against the brief.

First, look at the hard copy, if supplied. Has it been presented as requested? Usually that means double-spaced single columns in 10 or 12 point type. Check the e-files too – they should be in the software and include any coding you specified, of course – and remember to make a back-up file.

Next, check the length. If the index is much too long or too short, bear this in mind while you check the other points, as it might lead you to make suggestions for cuts or additions when you return it to the indexer to fix. Do not attempt to adjust the length of the index yourself: you are unlikely to do it as well or as quickly as the trained individual, and you could infringe his or her moral rights.

Now compare the index to the contents list to check that all major topics are covered. Have a look through the proofs to see whether there are any changes that will affect words or page references in the index. Make a list of these for the indexer, who will make the changes and check whether they affect other entries or cross-references.

Even though the index has been produced with the aid of special software, you need to check alphabetization and numerical order and style: information added after the list has been ordered can result in errors. And although the indexer should have used a spell-checker, you should make sure that names and foreign words are correctly spelled and indexed. You might also pick up words that are correctly spelled but wrong in context, such as 'cheery' for 'cherry', 'dive' for 'dove', or 'form' for 'from'. You will also want to check:

* the consistency of styling entries, locators and numerals;
* cross-references, to make sure they exist, use the same wording and are not circular;
* subentries, to ensure that they do not merely repeat the page references in the main entry or each other, and that they read back to the main entry properly;

- that entries and subentries have a maximum of about seven page references, as more is frustrating for readers;
- random entries to see that they use the same spelling as the text, are accurately located, and are substantive.

Exercise 6.4: Checking an index

Here is the briefing form sent to the indexer and a representative extract from the index to a book on archaeology (Fig. 6.2). The full index is about two pages over the required length. You do not have the text, so you cannot check the accuracy of the page references, but highlight any that you would want to check in particular. Assess the quality of work, listing your answers, with examples, under the following headings:
- Positive
- Negative
- Would check against text
- Would tell indexer to . . .

INDEXING CHECKLIST

Title: _____   **Author:** _____

Alphabetize
- ☐ letter by letter
- ☒ word by word

Capitalize
- ☐ all entries
- ☒ proper nouns only

Levels
- ☐ main entries only
- ☒ subentries
- ☐ sub-subentries

Layout
- ☒ broken off
- ☐ run on
- ☒ line space between sections of alphabet
- ☐ capital letter between sections of alphabet

Indent
- ☒ subentries _2_ spaces
- ☒ turnovers _5_ spaces

Locators
- ☒ page numbers
- ☐ paragraph numbers
- ☐ section numbers
- ☐ clause numbers

Punctuation
- ☒ space only after entries
- ☐ colon after main entries
- ☐ comma after main entries
- ☐ comma between subentries and locators

Numeral style
- ☐ full
- ☐ elided except for numbers ending in 0: 22–3 but 30–31
- ☒ all elided: 30–1

Reference to illustrations
- ☒ italic
- ☐ bold
- ☐ hyperlink
- ☐ other: _____

Special instructions
- ☐ chronological subentries for events
- ☒ exclude non-substantive references
- other: use – – for en rule

Extent
- _40_ characters per line
- _____ lines

Delivery
- ☒ hard copy
- ☒ by e-mail to you@your.iep
- ☒ software: Word

Figure 6.2 Index extract

Figure 6.2 Index extract (continued)

This exercise proves that you mustn't be fooled by appearances. Here, the presentation is good, but the underlying detail is poor. One of the few errors the indexer did not make is circular cross-referencing (e.g., 'axe *see* blade' and 'blade *see* axe'). On a real job you would check random entries against the references to make sure that the subjects appear where stated, that there is a continuous discussion where the references have been connected with an en rule (23–5) or independent mentions where separated by commas (23, 24, 25), and that they are substantive rather than passing mentions. Finding that one or two of, say, 24 random checks were unsatisfactory, you would check another random sample. If you found any more errors, you would return the job to the indexer to double-check the entire index and make all necessary corrections.

You would also have to consider whether the mistakes were so many and of such variety that you couldn't be confident that the indexer could bring the work up to the required standard. In that case, find another indexer and commission a new index. Do not give the new indexer the old index – it is the copyright of the person who created it, and it would not save time anyway. Reject the first index because it is of an unacceptable standard and explain that this is why you will not be paying the invoice.

Now you can see the importance of choosing the most appropriate person for the job, scheduling time for checking, having contingency time in case remedial work is needed, and offering a fee rather than an hourly rate.

7 Feedback

Acknowledging the work that people have done is an important way in which to build or strengthen relations for the future. Everybody can benefit from feedback, not just the people who report to you but you and all the people with whom you work, including authors and commissioning editors. Positive feedback reinforces skills, develops confidence and enhances morale. Appropriate criticism delivered in a constructive way can help people to improve. The absence of any feedback may leave colleagues believing, perhaps erroneously, that their work is satisfactory, or worrying, perhaps erroneously, that it is not. In either case they are likely to feel that they are not valued. Providing feedback is not only an important element in developing loyalty but also your responsibility.

Overcoming barriers

For many people in-house and for the majority of freelance workers, being given feedback occurs rarely or not at all. Why is giving feedback such a problem? Here are the top five 'reasons' people give for not providing feedback:
1 I don't have time.
2 Everyone makes mistakes and errors can be corrected.
3 I don't want to point the finger of blame.
4 I don't want to hurt another person's feelings.
5 I won't use that person again anyway.
   These are not reasons; they're excuses. Here's why you need to ignore them and set a better example of management.
1 No time? Providing feedback is an essential part of any manager's job, so no one can really be too busy to do it. You can work it into your schedule. It takes only a few minutes to acknowledge that work has been done well. Sending colleagues a copy of an author's thank-you letter or e-mail, or a photocopy of their names in the acknowledgements is a simple gesture that is greatly appreciated. Some publishers even send a copy of the publication to their freelancers.

2 Everyone does make mistakes, so project managers have to look at the nature and quantity of mistakes to see whether they are just occasional slips or evidence of sloppiness or ignorance or lack of a particular skill (see below). Correcting errors takes time and costs money, and it is wasteful of both to correct the same misakes repeatedly when they could be avoided instead.

3 The purpose of criticizing, of stating that something is wrong or below an accepted standard, is not to blame but to inform, so that the same errors can be avoided in future. It might mean that people will have to revise their working habits, update their skills, or learn something new. They will become better at their jobs as a result, which benefits them as well as those with, and for whom, they work. All of us can learn from our mistakes.

4 There are ways to deliver criticism constructively and tactfully. It is actually much more hurtful to leave people repeating mistakes, perhaps getting into bad habits that are then hard to break, instead of pointing them in the direction of improvement. It is, sadly, also often the case that people who do not criticize their co-workers directly will criticize them to other people. This is unfair and can seriously damage personal relationships, team spirit and the project manager's own reputation.

5 To decide not to use people again if they make mistakes is, of course, not possible if you and they are in-house. To take this attitude with respect to freelancers is wasteful of these valuable resources, limiting yourself to perhaps a very few who produce the work the way you want it the first time rather than building a team of people who can, with a little direction, do so subsequently.

Assessing errors

It is not enough to see that people have made mistakes; you have to determine what kind of mistakes. When there is evidence of more than the occasional, acceptable slip, look for a pattern or a common element. For example:

● Is the copy-editor poor at maintaining consistency, correcting grammatical errors, or marking-up?

● Does the proofreader fail to use appropriate colours or standard marks correctly, or fail to insert pages at cross-references?

* Does the indexer include unnecessary subentries or circular or blind cross-references, or fail to include useful cross-references?
* Does the picture researcher produce too few photos to allow a real selection, fail to reject substandard items before the editorial selection, or produce disorganized, untidy and incomplete documentation?
* Does anyone fail to meet the schedule, follow the brief, or communicate with you?

Then, particularly when there is more negative than positive to say about the work, review the individual's qualifications or experience: did you choose an appropriate person for the job? Next, review, as objectively as possible, the brief you gave: does it mention all the key points, clearly and unambiguously? Now you can decide to what extent the shortcomings lie in the performance and to what extent in the brief.

Exercise 7.1: Deciding where the shortcomings lie

Dave manages Body, Mind and Spirit projects for a large general publisher. He needed someone to copy-edit a guide to puberty for girls aged 10–15. He chose Sharon from the company's list of freelancers because the files showed that she has six years' experience as a copy-editor, has worked on general health and lifestyle books, and has always completed the work on time. He gave her the following brief:

> The book is a guide to puberty for girls. The text is 16,000 words, so needs a little cutting to bring it back to its intended 15,000 words. The caption allowance is an additional 500 words – not all the illustrations have captions. The author, Verity Bright, is a lecturer in medicine, so please make sure the text isn't too technical and that necessary scientific or medical terms are clearly explained. Verity's contact details are on the typescript and in the first e-file. We have agreed that you will return the edited files within two weeks and that the fee will be X. Please drop me an e-mail to confirm this after you have looked through the material, or give me a ring to discuss any changes.

Sharon confirmed the schedule and fee, and submitted the completed job on time. Checking the work, Dave noted that the text had been cut without the loss of essential information and that all specialist terms had been explained. However, he realized that the reading level was more suitable for an adult readership than his target market.

What kind of feedback is appropriate?

The hardest criticism to give and receive is self-criticism, but this is vital feedback for *you*, helping you to see how you can improve your delegating and briefing techniques. For example, perhaps, like Dave, next time you will check that the brief is more explicit. Or perhaps you will need to make the language clearer or check that everyone has the same understanding of the desired outcomes before the work begins. If, like Dave, you can see that the individual lacked the right skills or experience, you know that in future you will need to be more careful in selecting an appropriate person, or, if choice is limited by circumstances, compensate for perceived limitations by providing closer supervision and more support. Maybe you chose someone for their known strengths and this job is the first indication of their weaknesses; you can bear that in mind when you delegate another job. Admitting when the underlying cause of the mistakes is your choice of worker or an aspect of the brief will help you to frame your feedback in a fair and helpful way, and earn you the respect of your colleagues.

What to say

There are four possible general evaluations of work, which determine what kind of feedback to give:

1 The work is of the standard required in all respects.
2 The work is generally of a satisfactory or higher standard, but there are some points that need to be improved.
3 The work is satisfactory in some important ways but unsatisfactory in one or more vital aspects: those that could compromise the success of the project or make the work of colleagues more difficult or time-consuming.
4 The work is unsatisfactory in every way.

Criticism is easier to accept if it does not seem like a personal attack: be careful to describe the faults in the performance, not in the person. And always praise adherence to schedules and budgets.

1 *The work is of the standard required in all respects.*
A grateful acknowledgement that the work is satisfactory, and particular thanks for any aspect that was especially demanding or well done will not only be appreciated, but also help develop a good working relationship. In-house colleagues, who have no choice but to work with you, will be happy to do so and freelancers will want to; in both cases they will be careful to do good work and be productive because they know they and their efforts are appreciated.

2 *The work is generally of a satisfactory or higher standard, but there are some points that need to be improved.*
Start positively, acknowledging the general quality of the work and, as above, highlighting a specific element or two that were particularly important. Then it is easier for you to point out, and for the recipient to accept, that there were mistakes or shortcomings. Ending on a positive note puts the criticism in perspective, reassures colleagues that they and their efforts are appreciated and can encourage them to do better next time.

Exercise 7.2: Composing feedback

Now that the proofreading is completed, Belinda, the extremely busy project manager, is preparing to give feedback to the editor.

The brief for the editing had pointed out that the text needed a high level of edit to make it clear and readable, that the tables needed to be checked and marked-up for a consistent format, that the scattered editorial footnotes should be taken into the text, and that sources for items needing acknowledgements and permissions should be obtained from the author and given as end notes.

Because the editing was at a high level, the text was going to be rekeyed rather than corrections made to the author's files. Before she sent the edited text for setting, Belinda read some of the text that had been difficult to understand and concluded that Steve, the editor, had done a really good job of clarifying it without over-simplifying or losing the author's voice, and had edited the editorial notes seamlessly into the text. He had also complied with the other points in the brief, provided a separate list of items needing per-missions with their sources, and had maintained his reputation for returning work on schedule. The proofreading showed a small number of editorial mistakes, mainly an inconsistency in punctuating lists.

Draft notes that Belinda can use as the basis of written or oral feedback to Steve.

Steve deserves and will be given mostly praise. Belinda mentions the one editorial shortcoming; by referring to it as minor, she indicates her sense of perspective and reassures Steve while making him aware of an element about which he needs to be more careful. She ends with an even more reassuring note about working together in future.

3 *The work is satisfactory in some important ways but unsatisfactory in one or more vital aspects: those that could compromise the success of the project or make the work of colleagues more difficult or time-consuming.*
   Start by acknowledging what was well, or at least adequately, done. Then explain what was unsatisfactory and why, and what has to be done to rectify the situation now. Finally, indicate what the future holds. For example, when the individuals are in-house colleagues for whom you are responsible, you might state that you will ensure that they get training or that you will be supervising more closely how they work or use their time. For colleagues who are responsible to another manager, you could say that you will support their request for more training. You could make clear to freelancers that you will be able to use them again only when they can show that they have had training in the particular skill(s) in which they are not competent or on jobs that do not require the skill(s) at issue.

4 *The work is unsatisfactory in every way.*
   It is usually easier to spot, and therefore resolve, problems with in-house colleagues at an early stage because you might have more frequent meetings with them than with freelancers or because you are in the same place and might be aware that illness or stress is having an impact on their work. Depending on the length of the project, you might spot deficiencies in freelancers only at the end of their part of the job. If, based on the information you had, you

picked appropriate freelancers in each case and, objectively, the briefs were adequate, tell the individuals why the work doesn't meet the required standard. There's a slim chance that they have explanations (not just excuses), but you should make clear that if they don't, you will not use them again until they can show that they have been trained and are competent.

Exercise 7.3: Composing more feedback

Belinda has now turned her attention to preparing feedback for the proofreader.

The brief to Grace, the proofreader, was to read against copy, use standard marks in red to correct typesetting errors, in blue for editorial mistakes, and in pencil for essential queries. There had been an acceptable level of typographical errors. Grace had marked these in red pencil, and the small number of editorial mistakes in blue pencil, but used many non-standard marks and had not always used others in the correct way. The coloured pencil marks were not easy to erase, so the proofs looked messy in places where Grace had needed to revise corrections. There were a great many pencil queries, some concerning the acceptability of word breaks, others querying which spellings were to be followed when an inconsistency arose, but none on substantive issues. The work was returned on schedule.

Draft notes that Belinda can use as the basis of written or oral feedback to Grace.

Belinda acknowledges her own shortcoming in not providing the house style and reminds Grace to use her initiative. She provides practical advice about keeping proofs neat without commenting on specific examples of messiness, and, although she expects proofreaders to resolve word-break problems, accepts that not everyone else might do so; this is feedback to herself that Belinda can use to improve her briefing. So far, Belinda has tempered her criticism. However, the use of standard marks is so important that she wants Grace to brush up on this aspect of her work before entrusting another job to her. The implication is that Grace will get work again if she does as suggested, and the comment about reliable delivery reinforces that. Notice that the criticism is directed at the work, and comments about personal contact directed to Grace.

How to communicate

There are four ways to deliver feedback:
1 Face to face
2 By telephone
3 By e-mail
4 By letter: 'snail mail'
When you want to discuss something with a colleague, your options are 1–3 if you're both in-house, and 1–4 – but more likely 2–4 – if either of you is freelance. There are advantages and disadvantages to each, and sometimes using a combination of methods produces the best results.

Any method is appropriate when the feedback is all, or mostly, positive. Face-to-face is quick, and tone of voice and body language can emphasize positive comments and put negative ones in perspective. You can also see the effect of your comments and offer reassurance if necessary. When you and your colleagues are in-house, face-to-face is the first and best choice. It will do more to develop your working relationship than leaving a voice- or e-mail, which can have a distancing effect. When you or your team is freelance and face-to-face is not practicable, the telephone provides some of the same personal connection; in this case a voice mail shows that you tried for the personal contact.

In-house, a private meeting is the best way to deliver negative feedback. You and the team member can discuss why problems arose and what needs to be done now to resolve them, if necessary, or prevent them from recurring. You can use e-mail to set up a time to meet, but don't use it to deliver the feedback itself: it is too public and too impersonal. E-mail to freelancers can acknowledge receipt of work and indicate a letter is in the mail. Although criticism should not be put in the body of an e-mail, it can be put in an attachment, which is usually as private as a letter.

Although accepting all the reasons for providing feedback, some people are afraid to deliver criticism face-to-face. This inhibition can be overcome by being prepared. Don't try to deliver criticism spontaneously. Make notes on the positive and negative points, arrange them in a suitable order, and then practise out loud in a private place. Listen to your own voice and adjust the tone to be confident but not angry, firm not shrill, and reassuring where appropriate. Rehearse until you feel comfortable with the message and the tone. Then when you meet your colleague you will be more relaxed and confident. After a while, although you will still make notes about the points you are going to raise, you won't need to rehearse.

Do not deliver substantial criticism to a freelancer on the telephone. It is quite common for people to react defensively to criticism, and they might not be able to hear more than the first negative comment before reacting. There is nothing to be gained from an angry, argumentative conversation. Remember, too, that most freelancers work alone and might not have anyone to turn to for support.

Sending a letter has several advantages. It enables you to review all your comments before they are delivered, and revise them if necessary When you send your letter as an e-mail attachment, keep it in a draft for a while, then reread it before sending it. You want to be sure you have covered all the points, clearly and in the best order, and that the tone of the letter is objective. This private, written communication allows the recipient to avoid public embarrassment, to reread the comments in their entirety, have time to overcome the initial, defensive reaction and, it is hoped, accept accurate criticism and plan to improve in necessary ways. Sometimes it might be appropriate to indicate in a letter that you and the recipient should discuss the issues after he or she has had time to consider them. That affords freelancers an opportunity to explain or simply apologize, and to indicate what steps they are taking to improve, and it gives you the chance to offer or reiterate help, advice or reassurance.

There is no really good time to receive criticism, but consider your timing nonetheless. Getting negative feedback on a Monday can ruin the start of the working week, but will getting it on Friday or Saturday ruin the weekend or give a person time to consider it in a more relaxed or supportive environment before responding? Be prepared to listen to explanations, and to give people a second chance. However, know when to draw the line, and to tell the person concerned that you cannot use his or her services anymore, and why.

If even your considerate, balanced, constructive approach offends or is rejected by the recipient, you will know that you have done your best. Do not allow the other person's defensive reaction or ultra-sensitivity to upset you, undermine your confidence, or deter you from giving feedback in the future.

Remember, feedback can help you to improve your own working practices as well as make others aware of the need for improvement and, by reinforcing specific feedback when briefing for the next job, help them to avoid unnecessary errors. It will also help you to earn the respect of, and build strong relationships with, your colleagues.

Glossary

acquisitions editor *see* commissioning editor.

AIS Advance Information Sheets are produced as soon as a project is commissioned. They include the series, title, author, ISBN; specifications of format, extent, number and type of illustrations, style of binding; estimated selling price and publication date; a short author biography; a summary or short blurb about the text and, often, a complete list of contents; market rights available. They are a basic briefing tool for everyone involved in the project, from editorial, design and production to marketing, sales and publicity.

artwork A non-photographic image, it can be manually produced or computer generated; *see also* illustrations.

authors People who create text, illustrations, or indexes. Treat them with the same respect you have for, and expect from, all your colleagues. Remember, it is their project too, so keep them informed and involved.

blad A brochure of an illustrated book, usually 8 or 16 pages. It is the same format as the finished book, has the proposed front cover design, a list of contents, some representative pages of illustrated text, and a full specification. It is used to help pre-sell co-editions (*q.v.*) and as a domestic marketing tool.

brief The background on and instructions for doing a task. It should be concise, clear, complete, consistent, written and dated.

budget The money allocated to the project, a sum you must first check to ensure that it is adequate to achieve the quality (*q.v.*) required, and then one you must control and not exceed; *see also* direct costs, fixed costs, overheads, schedule, variable costs.

co-edition A publication by more than one publisher: book club editions, translations, and even same-language editions by another publisher in another country are examples of co-editions. Co-editions can be simultaneous or subsequent.

commissioning editor The person who commissions or acquires the project for the publishing organization. The title varies from company to company: commissioning editor, acquisitions editor, development editor, and publisher.

communication   It cannot be said too often or emphasized enough: this is the purpose of publishing and one of your primary responsibilities. If you want to succeed, initiate and maintain communications.

copy-editor   The person who edits the prelims, text and endmatter in detail, imposing house style and consistency; checking content for accuracy and consistency; ensuring structure and language are clear and at the right level for the intended audience; resolving ambiguities and queries; deleting unnecessary repetition; checking and styling notes, references, bibliographies and tables; checking that materials requiring it have copyright permissions and are given adequate acknowledgements; keying in illustrations; marking up text for designer/typesetter. May also be called editor, sub-editor or line editor.

copyright   The right of ownership of intellectual property. You must know its main principles and stay up to date with changes that affect its implementation. You must also ensure that the copyright of materials on which you work is protected and that permissions (*q.v.*) are obtained when necessary.

cover   Holds a book together. In the absence of a jacket (*q.v.*), it is the blurb- and information-carrying sales tool that makes the first impression on potential consumers.

critical path   The shortest sequence of events from the beginning to the end of an operation, an understanding of which is essential to planning schedules.

CTP   Computer-to-plate: printing plates are made directly from e-files.

desk editor   In some companies another term for project manager; in others, a copy-editor who reports to a project manager.

direct costs   The editorial, design and production costs allocated to producing the project; *see also* budget, fixed costs, overheads, variable costs.

dummy   A book of blank pages, made of the actual materials and to the correct size, extent and style of binding. Dummies are used by publishers to help sell co-editions (*q.v.*) before a work is commissioned.

editor   *see* commissioning editor, copy-editor, desk editor.

editorial project manager   The person who coordinates all the work in publishing a project. In some copmanies also called a desk editor (*q.v.*), particularly when working in-house.

e-file   Any electronic file.

feedback   Comments to team members about their work. Providing feedback is an essential requirement of a competent manager.

fixed costs Those direct costs that do not change no matter how few or how many copies of the project are produced; *see also* budget, direct costs, overheads, variable costs.

gross margin The profits a project might make if only it weren't subject to overheads (*q.v.*).

house style The styling of all elements of text and ancillary materials preferred by an organization; *see also* project style.

illustrations Visual images: artwork (*q.v.*), photographs, CT scans and X-rays.

indirect costs *see* overheads.

jacket Wraps around the cover (*q.v.*) and carries the blurb and other information about the book. This sales tool usually needs to be printed long before the book is, so project managers must schedule it accordingly; *see also* sleeve.

market The intended consumers – people – defined, for example, by age, interests, knowledge level and reading level; and countries into which it is intended the finished project will be sold. You must have this essential information at the beginning of the project, convey it to all team members, and ensure that the finished work is appropriate in all respects.

mark-up (1) a factor for relating the unit cost to the selling price; (2) codes used to indicate the nature of text elements for design and typesetting.

net margin The 'bottom line' on a proposal form; the profit a project might make after all costs are taken into account.

origination Scanning non-digital illustrations to produce digital files or films for reproduction; also called 'repro'.

overheads The costs of running the company that are borne equally by all titles, such as staff salaries and benefits; utilities; equipment, furniture, stationery; cleaning and maintenance; insurance and rent. It is seen on the budgets as a percentage of turnover; *see also* budget, direct costs, fixed costs, variable costs.

Ozalid A trade-marked name used generally to refer to final film proofs, which are also called blues, browns, and dyelines.

PaperlessProofs A proprietary name for software used to embed standard proof-correction marks in PDFs. The resulting PDFs can then be marked up using only Acrobat Reader.

pass for press Approving proofs for printing. Many editorial project managers pass the final revised proofs for press; others, who get to check plotter proofs or Ozalids, pass these for press. This book has assumed the former, as it is the more common circumstance.

PDF   Portable Document Format: retains all the design elements of the original e-file and can be viewed on any computer with Acrobat Reader, but can be altered only by using the software that created it, often Adobe Acrobat. It is used to send files to the printer for printing.

permissions   The agreement by copyright owners that their material may be used by someone else subject to an acknowledgement and, usually, a fee; *see also* copyright

plotter proof   A proof on paper of the imposition for printing plates, produced from e-files when printing will be CTP (*q.v.*). The proof shows all colours, but is used for checking position, not quality.

pre-press   The stages of book production before printing.

pre-production   The stages of book production before typesetting.

project style   Styling decisions for a particular project that are in addition to house style (*q.v.*).

quality   An element of text, design and physical production, ranging from high to low, that should be specified at the beginning of a project, so that the project manager can check that the budget (*q.v.*) and schedule (*q.v.*) are adequate, and can choose and brief the team members to achieve it.

repro house   The place where illustrations (*q.v.*) are made into digital files or film for reproduction; often a department in the printing house.

RSP   Recommended retail selling price.

schedule   The timetable for producing work. The project manager should create or check the schedule for every element of the project before work begins to ensure that it is adequate to produce the quality (*q.v.*) required, then ensure all team members are given schedules for their work, and monitor the project to ensure the schedules and budgets (*q.v.*) are maintained.

sleeve   The equivalent of a jacket (*q.v.*) for a tape or CD.

STM   Scientific, Technical and Medical.

unit cost   The cost of producing a single copy: the total production cost divided by the print run.

variable costs   Those direct costs (*q.v.*) that depend on the number of copies produced; *see also* budget, fixed costs, overheads.

Answers to Exercises

Exercise 1.1

text in
↓
copy-edit text
↓
typeset text
↓
first proofs in
↓
return first proofs
↓
second proofs in
↓
pass proofs for press
↓
e-files to printer
↓
make plates
↓
printing
↓
bound books dispatched
↓
books delivered
↓
publication date

Exercise 1.2

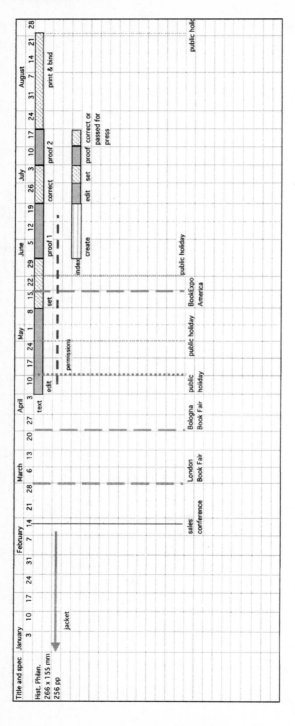

Exercise 1.3

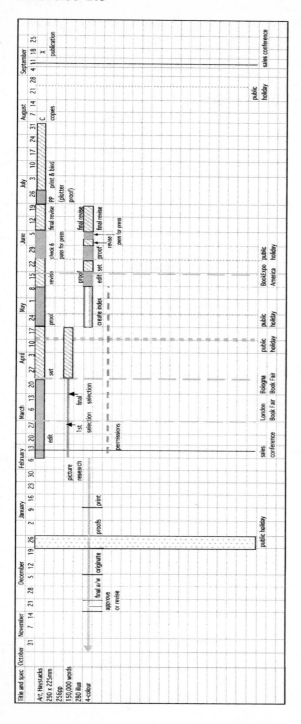

Exercise 2.1

	Moonlight Messenger	*Creating Scented Gardens*
Direct costs	author	author
	binding	artwork
	jacket design	binding
	paper and other materials	book design
	printing	copy-editing
	proofreading	indexing
		jacket design
		page make-up
		paper and other materials
		picture fees
		picture research
		printing
		proof corrections
		proofing
		proofreading
		scanning illustrations
		typesetting
Overheads	commissioning	commissioning
	copy-editing	project management
	page make-up	
	project management	
	proofing	
	proof corrections	
	typesetting	

Exercise 2.2

Fixed costs

author	proofreading
artwork	proof corrections
book design	scanning illustrations
commissioning	typesetting
copy-editing	
indexing	
jacket design	**Variable costs**
page make-up	binding
picture research	paper and other materials
project management	picture fees
proofing	printing

Exercise 2.3

1 Budget

turnover	50,000
direct costs	14,000
gross profit margin	36,000
overheads @ 38%	19,000
net profit margin	17,000
total expenditure	33,000
% net profit margin	51.5

2 Effect of couriers' bills on overheads

To find the percentage of overheads: $1500 \div 50,000 = 0.03 \times 100 = 3\%$
Couriers are already 0.25% of the overheads, so the effect on the
overheads is to increase them by 2.75%: $38 + 2.75 = 40.75$

3 Effect on net profit margin percentage:

turnover	50,000
direct costs	14,000
gross profit margin	36,000
overheads @ 40.75%	20,375
net profit margin	15,625
total expenditure	34,375
% net profit margin	45.4

Exercise 2.4

1 To find the unit cost, divide the RSP by the mark up:
   20 ÷ 6 = 3.33

2 To find the unit cost based on present estimates, divide the direct costs
   by the print run:
   73,000 ÷ 15,000 = 4.87.

   To determine the RSP based on this unit cost, multiply by the mark-up:
   4.87 × 6 = 29.

   Jan has not achieved her goal.

3

RSP	20.00
home trade discount (25%)	−5.00
	15.00
home sales	× 12,000
	180,000
RSP	20.00
export discount (50%)	−10.00
	10.00
export sales	× 3000
	30,000
turnover	**210,000**
direct costs	−73,000
gross profit margin	137,000
overheads 40% of turnover	−84,000
net profit margin	53,000
total income	210,000
ratio of net profit to total income	25.2%

Exercise 3.1

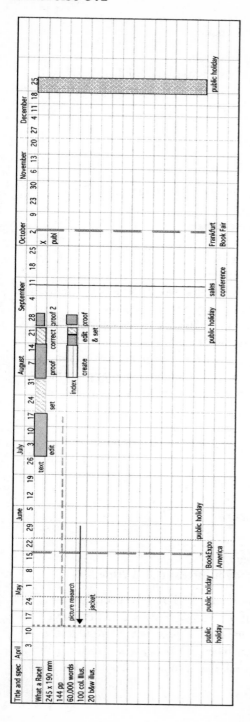

Exercise 3.2

These are the elements to notice:
* File labels are not precise
* Headings typed in different fonts and sizes
* Headings typed in caps, caps and lower case, and bold
* Text justified
* Text single spaced
* Text type size adequate
* Some text in italics
* Double-spacing after full points
* Embedded footnote
* Embedded tables and figure with directional references
* Photo suggestions in text
* Indented paragraphs and displayed matter

These are the points to note for the author:
* Label e-files by chapter, type of content.
* Type all headings capitalizing only the first word and any proper nouns.
* Type all headings and text in the same typeface and size.
* Do not indent any text: use a line space to separate paragraphs and to separate long quotations or other displayed matter from main text.
* Put footnotes, tables, figures and other illustration suggestions in separate files, not in the main text, and label those files appropriately.
* Number tables and figures separately and refer to by number in text, not above, below, etc.
* Spell-check the document before printing out.
* Change the format to double-line spacing before printing out.

Exercise 3.3

* Is it about the agreed subject matter?
    Yes, diet as part of health.

* Is it written from the agreed angle?
    Yes, scientific underpinning; myths revealed and dismissed.

* Is there evidence of all agreed elements, and no unexpected ones?
    There is evidence of information, self-evaluation questions and answers, diagrams, photos; unexpected footnote. Remind authors that book is for the popular market, so notes are not wanted. Where acknowledgements are required, they can be written into the text.

- Is source material adequately acknowledged and will permissions need to be cleared?

  There is incomplete information about the World Health Organization guidelines and no source for the weight table. Ask authors to supply complete sources for all tables and other acknowledged information. If tables are taken from other sources, permissions will need to be cleared.

- Is the draft text about the right proportion of the entire work?

  Each chapter would be roughly 12,000 words, which should include captions and running heads; at 1000–1100 words, this 10 per cent sample from a chapter is about right

- Is it well organized?

  Yes, so far, it proceeds logically from one point to the next.

- Is it well structured, with the appropriate number and levels of headings for the intended readership?

  There are sufficient headings, although the author's styling has confused the levels.

- Is the information at the right level for the audience?

  The text is simple and appropriate for the average adult, but check that use of only metric measurements has been agreed with commissioning editor and discuss the basis for that decision and the potential impact on sales.

- Is the text well written and interesting?

  Paragraphs are short, the text is in the active voice and the reader is addressed directly to maintain interest. There are some minor problems with spelling and typing (e.g., 'theirs' for 'there's', 'your' for 'you're', 'eight' for 'weight'), punctuation and consistency (all measurements given in metric, but text refers to 'extra inches' and 'shed . . . pounds'): mention in brief for copy-editor.

- Do tables, figures, notes relate well to the text?

  Yes.

Exercise 4.1

Text	Skill/quality
Popular level	Generalist editor
Minor spelling, syntax, consistency problems	Competent in basic skills
Incomplete source information	Good at spotting missing information and querying author
Tables, which might be from copyright sources	Competent at tables and will clear permissions
Figures need to be improved	Visually adept
Metric measurements	Might need to be able to convert to sensible imperial equivalents
Three authors	Good at discerning authors' styles and retaining individuality/making consistent; good planner and well organized

Exercise 4.2

Proofreader

Chosen	Not chosen	Because
Tom		Relevant training and experience
	Dick	Has relevant training and subject knowledge, but less experience and limited to articles
	Harriet	Has no relevant training, and no experience in books

Indexer

Chosen	Not chosen	Because
Zara		Relevant training, experience and subject areas at the right level
	Albert	Has training and experience, and works in some relevant subject areas but probably at too high a level
	Jack	Has no indexing training and has limited time availability

Exercise 4.3

Picture researcher

Chosen	Not chosen	Because
Michael		Looks for context and additional subjects, pre-selects for content and quality, is involved in project, has relevant experience and handles paperwork adequately
	Melanie	Relevant experience, good negotiator, but limits choice by requesting known pictures and pre-selecting 'best'
	Martha	Is experienced and efficient at paperwork, pre-selects for quality only, tries to prevent unnecessary charges, but works only to the list, is not involved in the project and does not negotiate

Exercise 4.4

Choose:

Claire to copy-edit on-screen with hard copy back-up marked up, prepare a/w briefs and check visuals. Total 145 hours. Claire would want 2900, but you could offer 2750, and be willing to negotiate to 2825, leaving 125 for minor expenses and a few additional hours' work if necessary.

Tom to proofread and collate. Total 38 hours. Tom would want 646, but if you offer him that, you will have only 24 for contingencies, or about one and a half hours' fee. Instead, you could offer about 590 and be willing to negotiate to 610, leaving up to 60 to cover postage and a few extra hours' work.

Zara to index. Total 30 hours, so Zara would want 600. You could offer about 540 and be willing to negotiate to 560, leaving 50 for minor expenses and a couple more hours of work.

Work you will do:

Cut and fill if necessary, brief the indexer and picture researcher, approve final artwork and picture selection, key in photos, clear permissions and write acknowledgements, edit and proofread index.

Exercise 5.1

Dear Claire

Here's to Your Health!

Following our earlier discussions, I am sending you the text and ancillary materials for this title, which I have itemized on the handover sheet; please check that you have received everything shown there and note which prelims are marked for you to originate. I am also enclosing the AIS, which summarizes the background information.

The text is an acceptable length and basically well written. In addition to giving it a light edit and sorting out the authors' inconsistent heading structure, please take the footnotes, or relevant parts of them, into the text; delete references to photos; and substitute figure numbers for directional references. Please put the mark-up and key in the figures on a clean printout. We have agreed that in preparing artwork briefs you will clarify and try to enhance the authors' rather basic and dull figures, add descriptive captions and delete any redundant text.

The authors have worked as a team and agreed that you should raise queries with Dr Spratt, who can be reached at [author's details and availability].

You said you can begin work the week of 17 January and we have agreed the following schedule:

* a list of details of any items requiring permissions during the week beginning 31 January;
* copy-edited e-files, original hard copy, and new printout, returned to me, ready for setting, by 3 April;
* a/w briefs returned to me by 7 February;
* artist's visuals to you 28 February, for you to check, correct if necessary, and return to me with the edited text.

You will e-mail the permissions list and text files to me and send the other materials by post. Please remember to update the handover sheet and complete the form for the designer, and enclose your editorial style sheet.

We have agreed a fee of 2825 for the job, plus reasonable expenses.

Please let me know as soon as possible if any problems arise with the schedule or the budget, and, of course, feel free to contact me about any issues relating to the project.

I look forward to working with you.

Yours sincerely

Title and spec	January				February				March				April			May			June				July	
	3	10	17	24	31	7	14	21	28	6	13	20	27	3	10	17	24	1	8	15	22	29	5	12	19	26	3

Here's to Your Health!
256 x 170 mm
304 pp
125,000 words
75 colour a/w
300 colour half-tones

text · assess · edit · proof 1; collate · correct · proof 2 · in & passed

permissions · list · clear

index · create · edit · set · proof

a/w · prepare briefs & check with author · prepare visuals · check visuals · prepare final a/w · check · set · check

project manager

sales conference · London Book Fair · Bologna Book Fair · public holiday · public holiday · BookExpo America · public holiday

Exercise 5.2

15 May

Dear Tom

Here's to Your Health!

I'm so pleased that you are able to do this job. Herewith the first page proofs, the editor's style sheet and the marked-up hard copy for text and captions. I'm also enclosing an AIS for general information.

Please use the established colours for marking changes and red also to key the missing photos into the appropriate blank spaces. The photos are not numbered in the book, so please check the keying-in numbers against those on the caption copy.

I will send you the authors' proofs for collation on 2 June, so that you can get all the proofs back to me by the 12th.

We have agreed a fee of 610 for the proofreading and collation. Please return all the proofs by special delivery. We will, of course, reimburse you for this.

Do get in touch if there are any matters you wish to discuss, and let me know as soon as possible if there are any problems with the schedule.

Yours sincerely

Exercise 5.3

15 May

Dear Zara

Here's to Your Health!

Here are the page proofs for you to index and a checklist of the main style points. Please follow the specification for the length of line and number of lines to ensure the index fits.

I'm glad you are able to fit this into your schedule. We've agreed that you'll deliver the files by e-mail and the back-up hard copy by post by 2 June, and that the fee for the work is 560. We will acknowledge your copyright in the index and your moral right to be identified on the copyright page.

Please contact me if there are any issues you wish to discuss or if any problems arise that would affect the schedule or your fee.

Yours sincerely

Exercise 5.3 (*continued*)

INDEXING CHECKLIST

Book title:_____   Author: :_____

Alphabetize
❏ letter by letter
☒ word by word

Capitalize
❏ all entries
☒ proper nouns only

Levels
❏ main entries only
☒ subentries
❏ sub-subentries

Layout
☒ broken off
❏ run on
☒ line space between sections of alphabet
❏ capital letter between sections of alphabet

Indent
☒ subentries __2__ spaces
☒ turnovers __4__ spaces

Locators
☒ page numbers
❏ paragraph numbers
❏ section numbers
❏ clause numbers

Punctuation
☒ space only after entries
❏ colon after main entries
❏ comma after main entries
❏ comma between subentries and locators

Numeral style
❏ full
❏ elided except for numbers ending in 0: 22–3 but 30–31
☒ all elided: 30–1

Reference to illustrations
☒ italic
❏ bold
❏ hyperlink
❏ other:_____

Special instructions
❏ chronological subentries for events
❏ exclude non-substantive references
other:_____

Extent
__30__   characters per line
__1300__   lines

Delivery
☒ hard copy
☒ by e-mail to [address]
☒ software: Word or RTF _____

Exercise 5.4

Book title: *Here's to Your Health!*   Author: Dr Spratt *et al.*

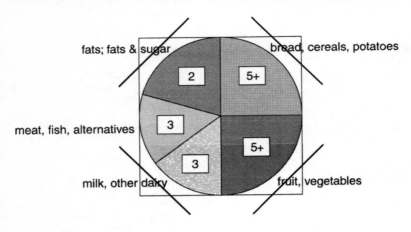

Figure 1
- repro size: ¼ page including anno
- omit squared background
- use symbols (e.g., crockery or food items) for number of servings in wedges, annotations outside

Fitness trail
- repro size: full page
- setting: outdoors, but do not obscure exercise stations with trees, etc.
- order of trail as shown, but scale each station approx. 100 metres from preceding one
- make arrow lines a wide path connecting stations
- add same human figure doing exercise at each station: see highlighted notes on reference
- add instruction boards near each station
- annotations free-standing, no boxes

PROJECT STYLE

Book title: _____

Author: _____

Illustrations
___ line
_2_ tone
___ black only
___ other monochrome colour _____
___ 2nd colour _____
_2_ full colour _____

❏ squared with rules
☒ squared without rules
❏ vignetted
❏ silhouetted _____
❏ bleeding
☒ not bleeding

_l_ representational
___ abstract
___ cartoon
___ realia
_l_ diagram

Working size
❏ ss
❏ × 0.5
❏ × 1.5
❏ × 2
❏ other _____

Annotations
☒ typed, marked-up list(s) attached
❏ plain lines to subjects
❏ arrows to subjects
☒ black only
❏ 2nd colour _____
❏ reverse out
☒ in separate file/on overlay

Electronic delivery
software _____
palette requirements _____

e-mail to _____
❏ disk format _____
❏ CD

Hard copy presentation
materials _____
_____

Schedule
Visuals by 28 Feb
Final a/w by 3 April

Exercise 5.5

Book title: *Here's to Your Health!*   Author: Dr Spratt *et al.*

For all photos:
- shoot in colour;
- models to be facing towards camera unless otherwise specified;
- head always facing same direction as body unless otherwise specified;
- models to wear form-fitting clothes, such as leotard and tights or T-shirts and straight-legged trousers, and to have bare feet unless shoes are specified. Colour of models' costumes must contrast with walls and floors.
- background: plain sofa or armchair, perhaps small side table, but minimal accessories and must not distract from main figure;
- props: where called for, must be stable – e.g., use desks, tables or sturdy chairs, not stools; if floors are wooden, use mats, not small rugs that can slide on surface. Avoid lamps, electrical cords, and placing any prop where model could bump into it or trip over it.

Shoot one photo for each caption, with model in position indicated by the highlighted portion of captions and notes.

Ex. 7 View model from right side
1 Stand leg length away from a thigh-high stable support, such as a desk or chest of drawers. Turn your right leg out slightly. Raise your left leg to the front and brace your heel on the support. Lean forward to grasp your heel with both hands.

2 Lean over and try to touch your forehead to your knee. Flex your foot for a count of five, point for a count of five, then flex for a count of five. Lower your left leg.
Repeat with the right leg.

> The model's head should not come really close to the knee – that discourages beginners. Complete body line is important; head is always facing same way as body unless caption says otherwise. Safety is important, so support shouldn't be anything that might tip when weight is placed on it. Alex

Ex. 8 View model from front

1 Stand with your feet just over shoulder-width apart, knees bent and toes turned diagonally out. Place you hands behind your head with your elbows back.

2 Bend your knees so that your thighs are as close to horizontal as possible, keeping your heels on the ground and buttocks tightened. Hold for a count of five, making sure your buttocks don't drop below knee level. Relax, then rise to your toes for a count of five, keeping buttocks and thighs tightened.

3 Lower your heels to the ground. Bend sideways from the waist towards your right knee. Hold for a count of five. Straighten, then bend to the left and hold for a count of five.

Ex. 9 View model from back

1 Standing straight or sitting on your bare feet, raise your left arm straight up and bend your elbow so that your palm touches your left shoulder blade. Press your right hand with palm forward against your left elbow and push your elbow back for a count of 10.

2 Extend your left arm straight above your head with your palm forward, keeping your right arm where it was. Stretch up for a count of 10, then return to the starting position.
Repeat with your right arm.

Title and spec	January					February				March				April				May					June				July
	3	10	17	24	31	7	14	21	28	6	13	20	27	3	10	17	24	1	8	15	22	29	5	12	19	26	3

Here's to Your Health!
256 x 170 mm
304 pp
125,000 words
75 colour a/w
300 colour half-tones

text — assess, edit, check, set, proof 1; collate, correct, proof 2, in & passed

permissions — list, clear

index — create, edit, set, proof

a/w — prepare briefs & check with author, prepare visuals, check visuals, prepare final a/w, check

photography — prepare briefs, shoot, check

project manager

sales conference

London Book Fair

Bologna Book Fair

public holiday

BookExpo America

public holiday

public holiday

Exercise 5.6

17 January

Dear Michael

Here's to Your Health!

I am looking forward to working with your on this project. Here is a copy of the text, a list of subjects and our standard picture research checklist. The subjects are broadly described and your creative input will be much appreciated. You'll see from the enclosed AIS that we need to ensure that the photos are suitable for an international audience, so please avoid those that are unnecessarily country specific: e.g., showing road signs, well-known monuments or buildings, or style of homes. We have agreed a fee of 2800, which will cover the two selection meetings shown on the checklist.

Do contact me if you wish to discuss any aspect of the list, and, of course, please let me know as soon as possible if there are any problems with the schedule or budget.

Yours sincerely

Picture list

Book title: *Here's to Your Health!*   Author: Dr Spratt *et al.*

1 Super-thin celebrities: internationally known models on catwalk, with established careers rather than this year's sensations.
2 People different shapes, sizes, ethnicity: a group shot if possible; must be healthy adults, not fat or anorexic.
3 Apple- and pear-shaped people: individuals.
4 People playing a variety of sports: mixed genders, ages, ethnic groups.
5 People eating healthy meals: healthy looking adults and children; visible food should include raw or cooked vegetables and potatoes, rice or bread; no deep fried or fast food, no evidence of smoking.

Book title: *Here's to Your Health!*   Author: Dr Spratt *et al.*

Picture researchers are expected to:

1 Pre-select photos for good reproduction quality.
2 Check invoices agree with fees and terms negotiated.
3 Provide complete and accurate picture credits for each image.
4 Package CDs or other materials to ensure they will not be damaged in transit.
5 Hand over complete and accurate documentation to the client at the end of the project.
6 Immediately inform the project manager of any problems that might affect the choice of illustrations, the schedule or the budget.
7 Provide receipts and records of expenses.

and for non-digital photos:

8 Check incoming materials and return damaged items to sources immediately.
9 Check delivery notes on receipt for accuracy and inform sources of errors immediately.
10 Keep a log to ensure location of materials is known at all times.
11 Take all necessary steps to ensure that holding fees are not incurred.
12 Return transparencies to sources after use, accompanied by an accurate delivery note.
13 Pay loss or damage fees for materials in their possession.

On this project you are requested to:

☒ research _100_ subjects in colour, _0_ in black-and-white
☐ acquire the specific photographs listed by _____
☒ acquire a sufficient number of photographs of the subjects listed for initial selection by __13 March__ and final selection by ___3 April___
☐ acquire photos that have not been published often
☐ acquire any relevant information for captions from sources
☒ negotiate copyright permissions and reproduction fees ___world___ markets and within the budget of ___1500___
☒ provide a complete and accurate list of picture credits for publication
☐ mark up a file copy of the book
☐ send materials by agreed courier service
☒ send materials by special delivery/registered post with adequate insurance
☒ liaise with _____[your name]_____

The client will:

1 Provide a comprehensive list of photographs required.
2 Provide a copy of the text when necessary.
3 Assume responsibility for the condition of materials while in the possession of its staff or subcontractors, and pay loss or damage fees incurred by any of these parties.
4 Comply with the terms and conditions agreed with the sources and pay their invoices on publication.

Gantt chart — production schedule

Title and spec	January					February				March				April				May				June				July	
	3	10	17	24	31	7	14	21	28	6	13	20	27	3	10	17	24	1	8	15	22	29	5	12	19	26	3

Here's to Your Health!
256 x 170 mm
304 pp
125,000 words
75 colour a/w
300 colour half-tones

text — assess — edit — check — set — proof 1; collate — correct — proof 2 — in & passed

permissions — list — clear

index — create — edit — set — proof

a/w — prepare briefs & check with author — prepare visuals — check visuals — prepare final a/w — check

photography — prepare briefs — shoot

picture research — prepare briefs — research — 1st selection — fill gaps — final selection — check

sales conference

London Book Fair

Bologna Book Fair

public holiday

BookExpo America

public holiday

public holiday

project manager

Exercise 6.1

A

1   Find out how much of the text and ancillary materials is finished.
2   Ask the author the cause of the delay; presumably she was still on schedule the last time you checked.
3   Explain the problems delay will cause, then say you'll have to see what you can do and will get back to her.
4   Consider whether work can begin on the material that will be available.
5   Assess whether the author needs two weeks, or more or less time to complete the outstanding work.
6   Work out the impact on the schedule and discuss it with the copy-editor and the design and production managers.
7   Contact the author with your response.

B

1   Phone the author. If no response, leave a voicemail and send an e-mail enquiring after the whereabouts of the proofs.
2   Check the author's contract to make sure it contains the standard clause stipulating that proofs not returned by the author on schedule are deemed passed for press.
3a If you get no response from the author, send the proofs for correction and inform him this has been done.

or

3b If the author says he sent the proofs two days earlier, ask him if he can recall any substantive changes he wanted to make. Record them and send the proofs for correction on time.

C

1   Thank the proofreader for letting you know and arrange for the proofs to be returned by the fastest means possible.
2   Assess whether there is sufficient time for one person to complete the job or if it would be possible and better to split it between two.
3   Consider how much of your contingency budget you might need to use if the only way to get the job done is for the proofreader to work unsocial hours.
4   Contact appropriate proofreaders until you find the one or two who can complete the work in the time available.

Exercise 6.2

Your list should resemble this one.

Checked	**Noticed**
• house style	• no comma in four-digit numbers, but consistent
	• imposed -ize, cap Earth, numerals for 10 and above
• headings	• restructure removes repetition, breaks up text helpfully
	• coded correctly
• punctuation	• corrected
• illustration references	• locations changed to figure numbers
• cross-references	• folio refs replaced with Xs
• moved paragraphs	• new order more logical
• first paragraphs for style and flow	• improved
• extent	• slightly shorter

Exercise 6.3

The proofreader has:
• followed the specific points in the brief
• used the standard symbols correctly and clearly
• raised only essential queries, clearly and concisely

Red corrections:
• many could be the result of program incompatibilities
• spacing in running head, poor alignment, missing indents are designer–typesetter's error

Blue corrections:
• relatively few
• no unnecessary changes
• three are for the same error – consistency of hyphenation – and so should be called to the copy-editor's attention.

Queries:
The query in the notes to the table points to a significant oversight by the copy-editor.

Exercise 6.4

Positive:
* presentation follows brief
* layout follows brief
* alphabetization OK and follows brief
* numerical order OK and style follows brief

Negative:
* Some entries and subentries are wrongly capitalized: boats: Medieval cog; copper: Deposits, Traded from Cyprus; Dendrochronology.
* The majority of subentries need prepositions or conjunctions in order to refer properly to the main entry.
* Some entries – adze, bone artefacts, burials, coins – have long strings of references and should be broken down into subentries.
* Some entries have unnecessary subentries: aerial photography, Anglo-Saxons, *Austrolopithecus*, bone, cacao, Chalcolithic, chopper tools, Copper Age, dendrochronology.
* Poor cross-referencing: the 'see also' for barley is blind (i.e., does not exist), and the expected cross-referencing is missing between 'adze' and 'chopper tools'; 'boat' and 'canoe'; 'bronze' and 'Bronze Age', and between both of these and 'Early Bronze Age'; 'calibration', 'carbon-14', 'dating methods' and 'dendrochoronology'; 'copper' and 'Copper Age'; and perhaps 'deer' and 'reindeer'.
* Inconsistent cross-references: 'Latvian dugout' is a subentry to 'boat' but 'Slav dug-out' is a subentry to 'canoe'; 'calibration' and 'dendrochronology' subentries to 'dating methods' do not have all the page references given in their main entries; 'coinage' is a subentry to 'China', but 'coins' is the style of the main entry and it does not include the exact page reference as the subentry.
* Inconsistency of style of entries: some are singular (e.g., bead, bone, canal, canoe, city) and others are plural (e.g., aboriginal societies, Aztecs, boats, bone artefacts, burials, burial mounds, coins, dating methods).
* Unnecessary entries: 'decree, Hellenistic city'; 'dendrochoronology' could be cross-referenced '*see* dating methods'.
* Abbreviations of place names: E. Asia, N. America.
* Mistyped page references: under 'boats', 'carrack 3133'; under 'copper', 'N. American groups 1225'.

Would check against text:
* Chou K'ou Tien to check spelling and determine whether it should be cross-referenced to and from 'China'.

* Unusual place names, e.g., Ahar, Çatal Hüyük, Deir el Medineh, Dejbjerg, Harappa, Kayatha, Kuala Selensing, T'ang.
* Personal names, e.g., Catherwood, Frederick (possible alternative spelling is Fredrick), Davis, E.H. (possible alternative spelling is Davies).

Would tell indexer to:
* cut index to required length by getting rid of unnecessary entries and subentries;
* create subentries where there are very long strings of references;
* check that all cross-references have an entry;
* create essential cross-references as example above;
* check entries in the singular form and change them to plurals unless they refer to a single object.

Exercise 7.1

Dave should deliver the feedback to himself. He should see that the brief does not mention the age of the target audience and does not state that the overall reading level is too high. Unless the text was clearly for young girls – for example, telling the reader 'this is what is happening to you' – the copy-editor would have no reason to question the level.

Dave should also notice that the information about Sharon in the file refers to 'general health and lifestyle' books; 'lifestyle' is not a term usually associated with books for children and adolescents, and there was no indication that Sharon had experience of working on books for that age range. Since Dave didn't tell Sharon to adjust the reading level, he doesn't know if she could have done so.

Exercise 7.2

Steve

Book title: _____

- Thanks for excellent job of making the difficult original text clear and accessible.
- Noticed particularly how you incorporated the footnotes into the text.
- The proofreading picked up some inconsistencies in punctuating the lists, a minor point/no one perfect/easily adjusted by the proofreader.
- Really appreciate the sources being given on the list of items needing permissions; makes my job simpler.
- Good to be able to rely on your producing such a good standard of work and keeping schedule as always.
- Look forward to working with you again.

Exercise 7.3

Grace
Book title: _____

* Thanks for doing a good job on picking up printer's and editorial errors.
* Sorry, I should have provided house style to enable inconsistencies to be resolved; feel free in future to contact me for information you need to do the job.
* Using correction fluid or tape to remove corrections is better than erasing, as it leaves cleaner, clearer background.
* Perhaps other clients prefer word breaks to be queried, but we expect proofreader to resolve unless there would be complicated knock-on effect.
* Appreciate the accurate job, but essential that only standard marks are used and in the correct way to avoid slowing down typesetter or introducing further mistakes; suggest brush up skills/go on course, then contact me again.
* Always appreciate work delivered on schedule.

Useful web sites

National Occupational Standards in Publishing (UK)
www.train4publishing.co.uk

PaperlessProofs
www.paperlessproofs.com

Organizations for editors
Australia
Society of Editors (NSW) Inc.: www.editorsnsw.com/
Society of Editors (Queensland) Inc.: www.editorsqld.com
Society of Editors (South Austalia) Inc.: www.editors-sa.org.au
Society of Editors (Tasmania) Inc.: www.tas-editors.org.au
Society of Editors (Victoria) Inc.: www.socedvic.org
Society of Editors (Western Australia) Inc.: www.editorswa.com

Canada
Editors' Association of Canada (EAC): www.editors.ca
Association canadienne des réviseurs: www.reviseurs.ca

Hong Kong
Women in Publishing Society: www.hkwips.org

Ireland
Association of Freelance Editors, Proofreaders and Indexers: www.afepi.ie

Netherlands
Society of English-Native-Speaking Editors (SENSE): www.sense-online.nl

South Africa
Professional Editors' Group: www.editors.org.za

United Kingdom
Society for Editors and Proofreaders (SfEP): www.sfep.org.uk
National Union of Journalists (NUJ): www.nujbook.org/freeln01.htm
Society of Indexers: www.indexers.org.uk
Picture Research Association (PRA): www.picture-research.org.uk

United States of America
Editorial Freelancers Association (EFA): www.the-efa.org

Index

Note to Reader
Locators with g after the number indicate an entry in the Glossary. Italic locators indicate an illustration.